Endor
The Coach AD...

"As leaders, if we truly want to make a dramatic impact on the learning and teaching that occurs in our schools, then we must fully embrace our role as an instructional coach. In *The Coach ADVenture*, Amy Illingworth (one of the best instructional coaches with whom I have ever had the privilege to work) peels back the layers of this complex work to get to the heart of what impactful coaching entails and the skills you need to do this work exceptionally well. She then meets you where you are and provides you with the practical tools you need to take the next steps on your own coaching adventure. You will benefit from hearing her story and learning from her commitment to **A**ppreciating the strengths in each individual, **D**esigning coaching plans that meet each person's unique needs, and the **V**alue she places on the collaborative partnership established with each person she coaches.

"In addition to sharing her own journey, Amy offers us the opportunity to choose one of two principals to follow as they embark on their coaching adventure, which gives this book a creative, fun, and insightful look at the very real challenges leaders face and the strategies they use to strengthen their own learning and become more successful in their roles as coaches. Designed to meet you where you are as a coach whether you are just starting out in the coaching role as either a teacher or administrator, you're frustrated that your coaching isn't producing the desired results, or you're a seasoned coach looking for some inspiration, *The Coach ADVenture* is for you."

—***Shelley Burgess,** co-author of* Lead Like a PIRATE

"Incredible wealth of information and insight into the process of becoming an effective instructional leader. This book is packed with relevant, practical, easy-to-follow information to increase your skills as an instructional leader. As I read this, I found myself wishing this book had been available at the beginning of my leadership journey. This will definitely be in my go-to books in working with new leaders and in furthering my own coaching effectiveness."

—***Amy Glenn,** teacher and former coach, Vista Unified School District, Vista, California*

"Dr. Illingworth has captured the essential components of leadership development, mentoring, and coaching to improve student academic performance, purposeful planning, and personal growth. It is definitely from the heart; her personal experiences and journey shared with the reader make this book different from others. Her evidence-based, tried-and-true research and implementation of the essential components herself provide the reader with strategies, questions, and opportunities for self-reflection and action development. *The Coach ADVenture* is a clever means to practice the skills from the chapters and help the reader wonder and reflect upon their own coaching style and practice. Whether you're a novice or veteran educator looking to improve student learning and achievement, this book is a must-read."

—*Dianna Carberry, EdD, retired assistant superintendent of leadership development and systems innovation, Sweetwater Union High School District*

"Dr. Amy Illingworth is an exceptional educator. Over the twenty years I have known and worked with Dr. Illingworth in education, she has proven that each and every educator and student can succeed with the proper support and learning opportunities. Students, teachers, principals, and districts have excelled under her leadership through her systematic planning and coaching. Coaching is and has been the key to her success! She is a skilled leader and knows what it takes to develop students as learners and masterful educators in a school system.

"Dr. Illingworth's book, *The Coach ADVenture*, has provided me with specific strategies, structures, and ideas for how to facilitate learning for my leadership teams as well as a clear instructional leadership plan for myself as I lead my school. What I also love about this book is the clear belief that each and every educator can succeed if given the proper coaching, and it gives you an outline on how to make that happen. This is a must-read for any principal or educational coach, and I plan to use this as an instructional tool for my assistant principal and teacher leaders."

—*Pauline Leavitt, principal, Ramona Middle School, Ramona, California*

"The Choose the Coach ADVenture organization really helps novice and veteran instructional coaches alike! As you adventure with the coach of your choosing, you encounter many coaching pitfalls. Choosing your own coaching adventure lets you address these pitfalls one at a time. Coaching can be overwhelming, but this book makes it so much easier to digest. Following Principal Martinez opened my eyes to pitfalls I hadn't even realized I'd encountered. Seeing how she addressed the problems was invaluable! I now have a much better handle on my own coaching theory of action. Illingworth reminds instructional coaches of the power of listening and asking the right questions. The examples and questions provided are exactly what I needed to narrow my focus for observations and coaching conversations. I've been in education as an instructional leader for over twenty years, and this is easily the best coaching book I've read. Illingworth gets straight to the point and helps coaches refine their thinking when observing and coaching."

—*Liz Wong*, *assistant principal, Montgomery Middle School,*
San Diego, California

"I have had the good fortune of working with Dr. Illingworth on many occasions. She has been instrumental in my growth as a principal. As one of the directors of the Aspiring Administrators and Professional Development team for our district, she consistently shared strong instructional leadership practices that helped shape our district's goals and plans to address them. In mentoring others, Dr. Illingworth created learning experiences that brought together theory with action; additionally, she consistently modeled these practices at the school site with administrators either through classroom observations or implementation discussions. In all cases, her advice and insights have been timely and effective. *The Coach ADVenture* is a conversation with the reader covering many of the instructional practices, belief systems, and organizational theory that she shared with our leadership teams. The book allows for reflection and application. I am sure you will benefit greatly as I have from Dr. Illingworth's insights and leadership experiences."

—*Dr. Ricardo Cooke*, *principal, Eastlake High School, Chula Vista, California*

"In reading Dr. Illingworth's new book, *The Coach ADVenture: Building Powerful Instructional Leadership Skills That Impact Learning*, I first and foremost appreciated Illingworth's attention to her audience. While some books approach the topic of coaching from strictly the author's point of view or background, Amy is sensitive to the fact that as school leaders, we are approaching this reading—let alone our professional development— from diverse backgrounds, experiences, and with different levels of instructional coaching. I thus enjoyed exploring the journey of Ms. Martinez from Learning for All High School, since I found her sections most relevant to my personal journey.

"Any educator can appreciate an experience where they can have a mental dialogue or ruminations with someone who doesn't necessarily provide all the answers but poses questions that lead us to greater understanding. *The Coach ADVenture: Building Powerful Instructional Leadership Skills That Impact Learning* represented the kind of experience that allowed me to ask myself questions and allowed me to take away what was relevant to my professional growth. In this exploratory approach, Dr. Illingworth models not only inquiry in this book of professional learning, she also models equity as she seeks to meet readers' needs at different points in their coaching journey.

"Although you can simply read one or two chapters from this book to take away something meaningful, this book kept hooking me into continuing on to other chapters that enhanced my understanding on instructional coaching."

—*Alex Salazar, assistant principal, Sweetwater High School,*
National City, California

the Coach ADVenture

BUILDING POWERFUL INSTRUCTIONAL LEADERSHIP SKILLS THAT IMPACT LEARNING

N
W E
S

AMY ILLINGWORTH, EdD

The Coach ADVenture

© 2019 by Amy Illingworth, EdD

This book is available at special discounts when purchased in quantity for use as premiums, promotions, fundraisers, or for educational use. For inquiries and details, contact the publisher at books@daveburgessconsulting.com.

Published by Dave Burgess Consulting, Inc.
San Diego, CA
http://daveburgessconsulting.com

Cover Design by Orange Brain Studio
Editing and Interior Design by My Writers' Connection

Library of Congress Control Number: 2019950003
Paperback ISBN: 978-1-949595-87-1
Ebook ISBN: 978-1-949595-88-8

First Printing: October 2019

Contents

Part IV: Finding Your Coaching Adventure **125**

Dedication

I dedicate this book to all the teachers, leaders, and instructional coaches I have known, worked with, and learned from. Every teacher and leader I've learned from was in this profession to make a positive impact on students and change the world one learner at a time. Please continue to work hard on behalf of each and every student we have the honor and privilege to serve in our schools.

I want to thank my family and friends for encouraging me throughout this process. Whether you asked me, "How's the book going?" or you read a draft of the book and gave me feedback, I appreciate your love and support.

Thank you to Shelley and Dave Burgess for their friendship, mentoring, and support before, during, and after the writing of this book.

Introduction

Most coaching and leadership books begin with a focus on students. After all, they are the reason we are all here, right? Every school or district mission statement includes a line about meeting students' needs, educating students, or building future citizens through our work with students.

Yes, students are why schools exist. And the ability to serve students well is often the reason excellent teachers are recruited, tapped, or otherwise encouraged to pursue teacher leadership, coaching, or administrative roles. But expertise in the classroom with students does not always immediately transfer to working with adult learners. When an educator takes on a leadership role, whether through formal or informal positions, the transition from the discussion about our work with students to the reality of our work with adults seems to get lost in the shuffle. That's why this book begins with a focus on leaders who want to enhance their instructional coaching skills.

First, let me clarify whom I mean when I say leaders. If you are an educator, I mean you. Every one of us has the potential to lead from where we are no matter our position or title. Teachers lead every day, in their classrooms with students, in Professional Learning Communities (PLCs) with peers, in staff meetings, and one-on-one conversations. Administrators lead every day as well.

Even though every educator is tasked with leading, few teachers or administrators receive formal training in how to coach other adults. Coaching for instructional leadership requires a skill set that includes knowledge of adult learning theory, an understanding of coaching models, clarity on educational pedagogy and student learning, and the ability to build trusting relationships with colleagues. I can say, from years of experience, that this is not an easy skill set to master. Each of these skills takes time, practice, and feed-back. The plus side is that it can be quite an adventure! We will dis-cuss each of these skills as we go on the Coach ADVenture together.

I began my career as a middle school teacher. A few years into my career, I was blessed to participate in a district initiative around a new-to-us pedagogy, It was a completely new way of teach-ing that required intensive professional development. Along with workshops, our school had a full-time peer coach who worked with us to support our learning and practice. After a few more years, I became one of those peer coaches, working alongside my col-leagues to learn and implement the new structure to support our students. Thanks to the encouragement of a principal who was my mentor and who is still my friend, I then stepped into an adminis-trative role. Since that time I have served as an assistant principal, a principal, a director, and as assistant superintendent at the district level, working at the elementary, middle, and high school levels. I've also had the privilege to work at the university level in an adminis-trative preparation program.

In all my roles in education, I have always thought of myself as a learner first, then a coach, and finally a leader. It is my desire to share with you my successes, my missteps, and my learnings throughout my coaching and leadership journey.

Throughout this book, you will find . . .

- A road map for your journey as an instructional coach
- Examples from the field, where I share my successes and failures on this learning, leading, and coaching journey
- At the end of each chapter, you will choose the Coach ADVenture you want to experience throughout this book. You'll read a little about two different instructional leaders and their schools, and based on the scenarios shared, you will choose the leader's next coaching adventure.

I see three paths on which you might be at this stage in your career. Each of these stages is ripe for a coaching adventure:

1. You are about to begin, or are in, a job that includes the role of instructional coaching.
2. You are a teacher leader who wants to improve your own practice and share your learning with others. You

recognize that you and your colleagues aren't getting much coaching, and you want to do more.

3. You are a site or district leader who wants to take on more of an instructional coach role; you support instructional coaches within your system.

A coaching **ADVenture** begins with an **appreciation** of an individual's strengths. From there, a coach collaborates with his or her colleague to **design** a plan that will help the educator transform his or her instructional practice on behalf of students. When completed, a coach has added **value** to a teacher's repertoire, and the duo can value and appreciate the work they did together. This is where our #CoachADV hashtag originates. I'd like to encourage you to visit and use this hashtag as you travel on your coaching adventure.

You will notice that each chapter's title is in the form of a question. That is by design. The art of questioning is a critical skill in the instructional leadership coach's repertoire. Asking questions is a powerful way to coach someone else to become their best self. An essential skill that pairs with asking questions is listening. Together, these skills will take you far on your coaching journey.

Now let's take a moment to get to know the two school principals we will be following through the coach ADVenture.

Principal Andrew Fox of Smooth Sailing Elementary School—Mr. Fox spent his teaching career teaching fifth and sixth grade. As a principal, he does not feel confident in his ability to support primary-grade teachers with their instruction since he's had no experience teaching lower grades; therefore, he often avoids going into those rooms or PLC meetings. When Mr. Fox does visit classrooms, he stands in the back of the room, stays a few minutes, then leaves. He does not write anything down, nor does he provide the teacher with any feedback.

The longer Mr. Fox is principal at Smooth Sailing Elementary School, the less his teachers respect him. Rather than stepping into the role of an instructional leader or coach, he manages from his office.

Learning for All High School—Ms. Martinez is a high school principal with experience teaching secondary English and English Language Development (ELD). Though she has never taught any math, science, social science, world language, or other non-English courses, she visits all classrooms on her campus regularly. In collaboration with her Instructional Leadership Team, she has developed a site walk-through form that she uses to communicate evidence-based feedback to her staff after each classroom visit.

While she may not be an expert at something like AP Calculus, she still has confidence to provide the AP Calculus teacher with feedback based on the site vision and agreed-upon instructional focus. Because she participates in the PLC meetings with the math teachers, she is aware of what the AP Calculus teacher is working on with his students, and she can provide authentic feedback based on what she observes in connection to the PLC discussion.

THE COACH ADVENTURE BEGINS NOW!

Each chapter, starting with this one, ends with an excerpt about each of the two principals. After you read the segment, follow the instructions to decide where their (and your) coaching adventure will go next. Let's get started!

Smooth Sailing Elementary School (SSES) has a professional development (PD) day coming up soon. Principal Fox wanted to hire a consultant to come and present to his teachers for the day, but his budget is tight, and his boss, the assistant superintendent, denied his request. Mr. Fox has never considered himself an instructional leader or a coach, so he is stumped.

What should Mr. Fox do next?

- To learn more about how Mr. Fox plans his PD day, go to Chapter One: Why Do We Need Instructional Leadership Coaching? This adventure will take you through Mr. Fox's instructional leadership journey from the very beginning. This journey is a great place to start if you are new to instructional coaching.
- To learn more about those to whom Mr. Fox reaches out for leadership support, go to Chapter Nine: Who Is in

Your PLN?

Learning for All High School's (LAHS) principal, Rachel Martinez, is looking to enhance her instructional coaching. She realizes she doesn't have a coherent, consistent system for her instructional coaching; in fact, she feels like she is running from class to class and PLC to PLC delivering feedback that is isolated from the other work happening around the school. After working with her own personal coach, Ms. Martinez is ready to build a coaching system.

What should Ms. Martinez do?

- To learn more about how Ms. Martinez develops a coaching system, go to Chapter Five: What Is a Coaching Theory of Action? This adventure will take you through Ms. Martinez's instructional leadership journey. This journey is a great place to start if you are already an instructional leader wanting to enhance your own coaching skills.
- To learn more about how Ms. Martinez worked with an instructional coach herself, go to Chapter One: Why Do We Need Instructional Leadership Coaching?

If you are an educational leader and an adventurer who would like to improve your instructional leadership coaching, I hope you will choose to keep reading! The beauty of our Coaching Adventure together is that you can travel in any direction that will support your professional growth. You can follow Mr. Fox or Ms. Martinez's journey, or you can use the Table of Contents as a guide to point you to an area on which you are focusing for growth. As you read, please consider sharing your learning with our educational community on Twitter, using the hashtag **#CoachADV** for the coaching adventure on which we are embarking together. For additional resources and reflection, visit https://reflectionsonleadershipandlearning.com/coach-adventure.

Part I
Developing Instructional Leadership Skills

Your coaching adventure may take you through this book chapter by chapter, or you may choose to jump around based on what you want to learn and experience. Either way, part one is dedicated to how coaches develop instructional leadership skills. A coach is not born; he or she is made through experience. If you are thrown into a new coaching role like I was, know that you are not alone! There are skills you can develop to support your work as an instructional leadership coach. You can come back to this part at any point as your coaching repertoire grows, and you need to develop new skills.

Chapter One
WHY DO WE NEED INSTRUCTIONAL LEADERSHIP COACHING?

In order to meet the needs of all students, we must also transform the experience for the adults who work in schools.
—ELENA AGUILAR

Think back to a time when you attended a mandatory full-day workshop as a teacher. You might not have been happy to be there. You spent hours the night before writing out detailed lesson plans so that a substitute could maintain control of your classroom and attempt to teach your students something in your absence.

Imagine that you walk into the large room and see theater seats where you will be sitting with teachers from a few other schools for the next six hours. You and your closest teaching friend find seats together and hope that you can do some planning throughout the day. The presenter starts with a funny joke and a silly video, so your spirits lift, thinking this could be a good day after all. Then the presenter begins to outline the topic. This topic, he explains, is research based and designed to help students achieve at high levels. As he explains this great new strategy that all teachers need to use, you whisper to your friend, "Isn't this what we've been doing for the past two years?"

She whispers back to you, "Duh! Wasn't this our school's focus all of last year?"

As the day continues, the presenter provides details about a teaching strategy that you are not only familiar with but one on which you have received other professional development and on which you've focused in your own classroom for an extended period of time. You get frustrated that the presenter never acknowledges the work you and your colleagues have been doing on this strategy. You look around for your principal, but he is not present in the workshop. You get bored with the repetition, and by lunch time, you shut down. After lunch you consider skipping the afternoon session but realize you might "get into trouble," so you show up, only for the presenter to repeat part of his morning session again.

When the day ends, you are tired, even though you've done nothing but sit and listen all day. You are annoyed that you wasted an entire day away from your students for nothing new. You are angry that your principal wasn't there to realize that the entire workshop was a repeat of what your school had already been doing. And you realize that you and your friend didn't even have any time to talk about lesson plans together throughout the day, so now you must spend time outside of your professional development day collaborating for upcoming lessons.

Now imagine a different scenario: You are a teacher, and you've determined that one of your professional goals for the year is to learn about different ways to structure student talk so that all your students use academic language in meaningful ways throughout class. You have been reading books, articles, and blogs about the topic. You've tried a few ideas in your classroom, but you are feeling stuck with the lack of progress. Then you realize there is a resource on your campus that you haven't turned to yet: the instructional leadership coach.

You schedule a meeting with the coach to talk about your goal and what you've done. Your coach asks you a number of reflective questions that get you thinking about your students' strengths and areas of need in the upcoming unit. Together you collaborate on a structure you can build into your next lesson plan. At the end of your planning session, which was guided by your coach's questions that forced you to think deeper about the topic, you feel okay but not quite confident. Your coach offers to come co-teach the lesson with you, so you both can see the students in action. You happily accept his offer, and you plan who will do each part of the lesson to try out this new student talk structure.

After the lesson, you meet to discuss what went well and what didn't work. Your coach was able to capture the specific language he heard some of your students using during the lesson, which helps you see that the strategy was successful for a large group of students. Together you discuss what revisions you should make to help the students who haven't yet been successful. You commit to trying the revisions the next day, and your coach offers to come back to observe. You invite him back anytime because you appreciate a second set of eyes and ears in the room. After the next lesson, he shares with you his observation notes and asks you questions to consider for next steps. Through his questioning, you make decisions about how to move forward with your structured student talk strategies, and you have evidence to support the progress you are making on your professional goal.

Based on the two scenarios above, which teacher learned something that impacted his or her instructional practice? Which teachers' students benefited from the learning that took place? Which scenario had instructional leadership coaching built in?

These scenarios are based on real experiences I've had. Obviously the second scenario is more beneficial for the teacher as well as the students. In the first scenario, the adults sit passively, with no choice in their own learning and no support or accountability afterwards. In the second scenario, the adult learner has a voice and choice in the learning topic and the outcome, there is support and reflection built in through the coach, and the learner is more committed to a successful outcome, using the new strategy.

These scenarios illustrate why schools and districts need to offer instructional leadership coaching. If the goal is to impact student learning, the first step toward that goal is to make positive changes to the teaching practices used in classrooms. Teachers already work hard on their own. As leaders (be it a teacher leader, coach, or an administrator), we want to enhance the great work our colleagues are already doing through a side-by-side coaching approach that provides instructional leadership support.

Principals and teacher leaders with instructional leadership coaching skills can provide that side-by-side support to the hard work teachers do. While principals typically have many additional duties on their plates, few would argue about the importance of supporting teachers so that all students can be more successful. And in the age of budget cuts, many schools and districts do not have the ability to hire instructional coaches to serve in this role. It is therefore even more important that site leaders (principals, assistant principals, deans, and teacher leaders) build their own instructional leadership coaching skills.

CHOOSE THE COACH ADVENTURE

If you have just arrived from the Introduction and are curious about those to whom Mr. Fox reaches out for help as he dives into planning a PD day with his staff, or you've come from Chapter Seven where Mr. Fox was learning how to listen, keep reading about Principal Fox.

If you've just arrived from the Introduction, where you learned that Ms. Martinez worked with her own coach, skip down a bit to continue the journey with Principal Martinez.

PRINCIPAL FOX

When we last left Principal Fox, his request to hire an outside consultant for an upcoming professional development (PD) day had been denied. His boss advised him to consider his site's needs and his teachers' expertise when planning a PD day that would benefit them directly.

Principal Fox decides to try a new approach for planning this PD day. He goes straight to his teachers, specifically his grade-level leaders. He calls a meeting with the leaders of each grade level and begins by asking them each to name what they believe the school's focus has been this year. (He read about this idea in *Lead Like a Pirate: Make School Amazing for Your Students and Staff* by Shelley Burgess and Beth Houf.) As they go around the table sharing, it becomes evident that each teacher has a different idea. Some ideas that are shared include support for English Learners, student talk, academic language, increasing parent engagement, and math.

After listening to each person, Principal Fox takes time to address what they all just heard. He says to the group, "Wow. This is an important learning opportunity for me. Hearing you each mention something different makes me realize we need to work on clarity. Our school needs a clear direction and a focus on which we are all working together. It seems like our upcoming PD day might be a good time to get some clarity. What do you think?"

For the next hour, the group discusses activities they could do with the entire staff during the PD day. Teachers who have never spoken in front of their peers are volunteering to facilitate parts of the day. Principal Fox feels uncomfortable releasing so much control over to the teachers, but as they continue to plan, he sees their excitement, and their energy helps him realize how valuable this PD can actually be for the entire staff.

After the meeting, Principal Fox takes time to reflect in his office. He realizes that hiring an outside consultant would have been a really bad idea for his staff right now. Instead of bringing in yet another new idea, he has crafted an agenda for the PD day that was co-created with his teacher leaders. It considers where they have been, what their students need, and for what their teachers have been asking: time to collaborate around a common focus. He believes that after this day, his site will have clarity around one or two key initiatives on which their entire site will focus and that his teachers will have time with their colleagues to collaborate on planning lessons to meet their students' needs.

- To learn more about how Mr. Fox's PD day goes, go to Chapter Three: What Is the Role of an Administrator as Instructional Leader and Coach?
- To learn alongside Mr. Fox as he learns to build capacity and share responsibility, go to Chapter Four: What Is the Role of a Teacher Leader as an Instructional Coach?

PRINCIPAL MARTINEZ

Ms. Martinez, the principal of Learning for All High School (LAHS), considers herself a strong instructional leader. She knows a lot about pedagogy and feels that one of her most important roles as principal is to serve as the lead learner on her campus. When she first got her principalship, she reached out to a mentor who could serve as a coach for her.

Meeting monthly with her coach, Ms. Martinez came to realize how she needed to do more than be visible on campus; she needed to be in classrooms and teacher meetings, working alongside teachers and providing meaningful and timely feedback about instruction in order to see improvements in student learning. Ms. Martinez and her coach discussed how she could communicate her role as a coach with her staff and what her schedule would look like. In her principal meetings, she got the sense that very few of her colleagues were in classrooms regularly and that they filled up their days with office work. Unfortunately, she knew of one colleague who sometimes left school even before the students did, so he could make a standing golf game. Ms. Martinez knew that her frequent presence in classrooms would be a change for her teachers, and she wanted to effectively communicate what she would be doing and why.

Through multiple conversations, her coach asked her reflective questions that pushed her thinking further and helped her design her approach. She began by sharing an article on pedagogy with her staff at a meeting. As they discussed the article, Ms. Martinez explained that she took her job very seriously because she was ultimately responsible for ensuring that all LAHS students learned and achieved at high levels. The only way she would be comfortable speaking about that would be to see student learning in action, which would mean that she would be visiting classrooms regularly. While in classrooms, she would be noticing the effective pedagogical strategies used by the staff as well as where and when students were successful. She explained that she would share her observations with the staff, so they could continue to have instructional discussions personally as well as in their PLCs and as a whole staff.

She began to visit rooms and provide feedback in person as much as possible and in writing when she couldn't connect with a teacher within twenty-four hours. She also made sure to highlight teachers' strengths in her messages.

- To learn more about how Ms. Martinez defined her role as instructional coach, go to Chapter Three: What Is the Role of an Administrator as Instructional Leader and Coach?
- To learn more about how Ms. Martinez approached coaching, go to Chapter Six: What Does Coaching Look Like?

Chapter Two
WHAT ARE INSTRUCTIONAL LEADERSHIP COACHING SKILLS?

*Change begins with a culture where everyone
is elevated to the status of learner.*

−SARAH BROWN WESSLING

As we saw in Chapter One, instructional coaches can collaborate with teachers to help them develop and hone strategies that impact student learning.

Instructional coaches need knowledge of adult learning theory, an understanding of coaching models, clarity on educational pedagogy and student learning, and the ability to build trusting relationships with colleagues. An instructional leader is an educator who knows content and pedagogy and who is able to have constructive, evidence-based feedback conversations with other educators about content and pedagogy to improve student learning. These conversations may be one-to-one after a leader visits a classroom formally or informally, or they may be within a professional learning community (PLC) or grade-level meeting where teachers are collaborating on designing instruction based on students' needs.

It is important for instructional coaches to understand the differences between how adults learn and how children learn, but when I made the transition from teacher to coach and then administrator, I didn't know much about adult learning theory. Over time

I learned through reading the research and through some of my own missteps from bad meetings or workshops I attended, that I felt as if the presenters were speaking down to me.

Adults come to any new learning situation, whether it is a workshop, a staff meeting, or a coaching conversation, with many years of experience and internalized motivations to learn. If the new learning is not set into the adult's current context, it seems irrelevant to the adult learner. Think about the scenario in Chapter One when the teachers attended the mandatory professional development workshop. The teachers had previous knowledge of and experience with the "new strategy" being shared by the presenter. Their background knowledge, however, was never acknowledged nor taken into consideration during the presentation. They left feeling frustrated and without any new relevant ideas that could impact their students' learning.

As an instructional coach, it is important that you understand these elements of adult learning theory and build them into any learning opportunities you plan with your staff.

Instructional coaches must also understand coaching models. If you Google "instructional coaching models," you will see about eight hundred thousand hits. Within those findings, you will see names of well-known authors Jim Knight and Elena Aguilar, two experts in this field from whom I have learned a lot through their books, articles, blogs, and tweets. Through my readings of Knight's work, I have recognized the value of listening and understanding a theory of action, the concept that builds the *what* and *why* of coaching. Through Aguilar's work, I have learned the importance of emotional intelligence, relationship and trust building, and how equity can bring about a new level of coaching conversations.

As an instructional coach, you need to know what coaching model you will use. Ideally, you will be situated within a system that supports instructional coaching and provides you a model. In the real world, many of us must attempt to do this work in isolation because our system hasn't caught up to us yet.

We will talk more about designing your own coaching model and theory of action in a later chapter. For now, take a moment to reflect on these questions:

- Why do you want to be an instructional coach?
- What is your school's or district's vision for coaching?
- How will your teachers, students, school, or district benefit from instructional coaching?
- Will everyone receive the same amount and level of coaching? If not, how will you differentiate?
- Is working with you as a coach voluntary or mandatory?

Once you've established your instructional coaching model, you also need clarity on educational pedagogy and student learning. As a site or district leader, it is important that you determine what your instructional focus will be for the year. This focus should be based on your goals (through your site plan, strategic plan, Local Control Accountability Plan if you are in California, etc.) and should be clearly communicated to your staff. Throughout this book, you will read about examples where a goal was or was not communicated clearly to staff members and the benefits and challenges that occurred as a result. Focus and clear communication are essential!

We can't have a goal to "improve student achievement" without narrowing our focus. What part of student achievement do we want to improve? Is there a specific content area where our students struggle? Within that content, which skills or strategies do our students find challenging? What data are we using to make these determinations? This becomes a skill in and of itself as you learn to drill deeper into data, manipulating it until you can answer all your questions. From the statewide test results that are published in a newspaper down to the individual student report level that differentiates a student's strengths and areas for growth, data tells us a lot when we know where and how to look.

With a clear focus in mind, we need to determine which instructional practices will help our students grow in the specific area we have selected. These are the instructional practices in which we provide professional development and support for teachers. Once teachers have been exposed to a new practice, instructional coaching can be the follow-up support to help teachers learn to master the practice with their students. It may seem simple enough to just tell people what the initiative is, but the knowing-doing gap between what we think teachers know (because they sat in a workshop listening to someone talk about an idea) and what they do (when we observe them and don't see that workshop idea in action) can be wide. A combination of adult learning theory applied to your professional development and individualized instructional coaching can close the knowing-doing gap.

Consider the following questions from your own context:
- What is (are) your school's student achievement goal(s)?
- What are your district's student achievement goals?
- What specifically do you want to see students saying or doing that they aren't yet saying or doing?
- What instructional moves can teachers plan to help students meet those goals?
- What supports have you provided teachers around those instructional moves?
- Does your system have clarity around what the instructional moves look and sound like in planning and delivery?

The teacher from the second scenario in Chapter One had a clear focus: He wanted to improve his students' use of academic language during structured talk opportunities. With this clarity, he was able to research possible strategies and ask his instructional coach for specific support. The coach was able to collaborate with the teacher to provide the support the teacher wanted and needed in order to help his students be more successful.

A WORD ON OBSERVATION AND NOTETAKING TOOLS

As a coach, you will be observing a lot of lessons. Don't feel you have to be a content expert in every subject taught at your school. Your role as a coach is to facilitate the growth and development of peers, who do have the content expertise, and to support their learning of new pedagogy that will help them reach their students. A variety of tools are available for taking notes during an observation, so choose one that meets the needs of your coaching work. If you are working with a teacher who is struggling with classroom management, for example, you want to be able to take note of what student behaviors occur, which of those behaviors the teachers addresses, and any behaviors the teacher does not address. It might be helpful to keep track of which students shout out answers or get out of their seats and how the teachers addresses misbehaviors. [See Appendix A for sample note-taking guides.]

You could be in a very different coaching situation with a teacher who wants to improve her questioning techniques. A simple T-chart note-taking guide might work well. If you keep track of the teacher's questions on the left and how students responded on the right, you can use your notes to have a coaching conversation with the teacher. As a coach, I would often write down as much as possible while observing in a room, then I would make a copy of my notes for my discussion with the teacher. In this case, I might ask the teacher to read through the notes, then I might ask some of the following questions:

- What types of questions did you ask?
- What kinds of responses did you hear from students?
- Which student response demonstrated mastery (or what you wanted to hear)?
- What type of question got that response from students?
- What student response surprised you?
- Was there something you wanted to hear from students that you didn't hear in this lesson? If so, how might we craft a question or task to elicit that response?

Sometimes you begin a new coaching relationship by observing a classroom just to get a feel for the teacher's style and how students respond to him or her. I often have colleagues ask me, "What do you look for in classrooms? How do you notice so many different things?" First, I remind them that I have had many years of practice as an instructional coach. It takes a long time to hone your observation skills. This coaching work is an evolving process for us all!

Before I share with you some of the things you might observe in a classroom, let's take a moment for a quick journey together. Let's visit a classroom at Principal Martinez's high school from our Choose the Coach ADVenture. Imagine that you and I are doing a walkthrough with Principal Martinez. She decides to take us into a tenth-grade math class. Here is what we observe:

As we walk into the classroom at 10:25, we notice there are thirty-two students. The students are sitting in desks that have been moved to form groups of four. The students have notebooks open in front of them as well as their math textbooks. The teacher is standing in front of the class using her iPad to write and project her work on the front board for students to see. On the board is a problem the teacher has just finished working on. Nothing else is written on the board. At 10:30 the teacher tells the class they should work on the next problem. She says they can work with their group. The students begin to work. At 10:31 there is total silence in the room.

I walk up to one student, lean down, and whisper, "What are you learning today?" The student looks up at me and whispers, "Math." I continue, "Yes, I know we are in your math class, but what specifically are you learning today?" The student begins to squirm, and he points down to his notebook and says, "We are doing this." I look at the book, and I see quadratic equations. I whisper, "I see that this section is about quadratic equations. What can you tell me about quadratic equations?" The student mumbles something I can't hear, then the student sitting next to him pipes up with a definition of quadratic equations. I thank that student, and I step back from the group.

The three of us walk around the room, and I ask a few more students what they are learning and have similar conversations. At 10:45 we exit the classroom and step outside to debrief what we saw. I ask you and Principal Martinez what I always ask when I leave a room: "What can we celebrate? What is going well for students in that room?"

Principal Martinez shares with us that the teacher is using the adopted curriculum, which has been a struggle in this department. She also shares that she likes the fact that the students are sitting in groups. I pause here to push back on the language of "I like . . . ." I explain to you both that if we were giving this teacher feedback right now, and we said, "Your principal likes when the students sit in groups," she would have it in her head that she needs to have group seating whenever the principal comes in. Instead of worrying about how to impress the principal, I want the teacher to know why group seating is beneficial for student learning; therefore, if we were talking to her, I might say, "I appreciated that your students' desks were moved to create a group structure. When students have opportunities to work with their peers, they can develop their speaking and listening skills, their use of academic language in context, and their ability to problem solve and collaborate."

After we share some celebrations, I ask you and Principal Martinez, "What else did you notice? What wonderings do you have?" We were only in the room for about fifteen minutes, so we can't make assumptions, but we can generate wonderings about which we could talk to the teacher in a future coaching conversation. You look to me and say, "I wasn't a math teacher; I'm just not sure what to look for in a math class." I thank you for your honesty and remind you that you have pedagogical knowledge and that even without content expertise, there is a lot to see in a class; for instance, how many students spoke during the fifteen minutes we were in the room? You say that the only student voices we heard were when I spoke directly to students. "Exactly," I say. So that makes me wonder about when and how students are given the opportunity to speak in this class. It also makes me wonder if there are roles or a structure for group work. When the teacher told the students to begin working, she said they could work with a partner, but none of the students did that. Have they had prior partner or group experiences in this class? Are there group roles that students know or to which they could be exposed that would help them work together as a group?

This is just a snapshot of what I look for and think about when I visit a classroom. Below is a list of possible instructional, environmental, and cultural items you might observe in a classroom:

INSTRUCTIONAL

- Number of students present
- Number of girls vs. boys (though I caution you to be careful with this as we move into a less binary gender world)
- Number of students by race or ethnicity, English learner status, etc.
- Break down of minutes of teacher talk, student talk, and silence
- Learning tasks—What are students actually saying or writing?

- Daily objective or learning target—What is stated or posted about the day's learning?
- Text—What text(s) are students seeing, using, reading, or viewing?
- Cognitive load—Who is doing the thinking?
- Academic language—What academic language do you see or hear students using in their writing or their original speech?
- Standards—Do the learning tasks align with grade-level standards? Do they align with school and district curriculum expectations?

ENVIRONMENTAL

- Room setup—Students' seating arrangement, teacher desk, other furniture, etc.
- Print-rich—Are there books, posters, or charts visible in the room?
- Student work—Is there current student work visible in the room?

CULTURAL

- Representative—Do the posters, pictures, or books in the room reflect the culture of the students? Do they reflect diversity?
- Risks—Do students feel comfortable taking risks?
- Relationships—Are students smiling? Does the teacher address students by name? Do students address each other by name? Do you hear respectful language spoken?

The best advice I can offer a coach in an open-ended situation like this is to stick to your school's focus area(s). You can walk into a classroom and notice a million different things, but you will not be an effective coach if you attempt to talk about one million ideas with a teacher. You want to narrow your lens, so you can coach into a familiar area.

Another tool in the instructional coaching toolbox is the ability to build trusting relationships with colleagues. It is well worth your time to invest in getting to know your staff early on and letting them get to know you. Discover and celebrate their strengths. Once people know you are there to support them and are not "out to get them," they will work with you to learn more to benefit students. We will explore the importance of taking time to listen as you build relationships in a future chapter.

Armed with adult learning theory, an understanding of coaching models, clarity on educational pedagogy and student learning, and the ability to build trusting relationships with colleagues, you can start your instructional coaching journey!

CHOOSE THE COACH ADVENTURE

If you have just arrived from Chapter Six, and you are curious about how Mr. Fox develops instructional coaching skills to work with his primary teachers, keep reading.

If you've just arrived from the Chapter 3 and want to learn how Ms. Martinez helps her teachers understand her coaching role, skip down a bit to continue the journey with Principal Martinez.

PRINCIPAL FOX

Our elementary principal colleague, Mr. Fox, just wrapped up his first coaching cycle with a fifth-grade teacher. While he was excited after this successful interaction, he was still nervous about trying a coaching cycle with a primary-grade teacher. Before attempting that, Mr. Fox decided he needed to practice observing and providing more strength-based feedback in his primary classrooms.

For two weeks, Mr. Fox visited his primary classrooms every day. He began to leave small notes, highlighting a strength he observed. Then he added a reflective question at the end of his notes. At the end of the two weeks, one of his grade-level lead teachers asked to meet with him.

The teacher came into the meeting looking nervous. Mr. Fox asked her, "What's up?" The teacher said, "Some of the teachers are wondering why you are picking on the primary grades."

Mr. Fox was dumbfounded. "Picking on them? What do you mean?"

The teacher went on to explain that the staff had been comparing notes, and they realized that he had spent a week and a half working with one fifth-grade teacher then at least ten days observing all of the primary teachers every day, while he hadn't been to some of the other upper-grade teachers at all. She said that the staff was feeling like he was out to get the primary teachers and that his notes were beginning to sound like they had done something wrong.

Mr. Fox tried to explain what he was doing and that he was learning how to be an instructional leader. But at the end of the conversation, both he and the teacher felt uncomfortable. He didn't think anything had been resolved, and he was now nervous to visit any classroom.

- To learn about Mr. Fox's next steps to address his teachers' concerns, go to Chapter Twelve: How Do Coaches Address Challenges and Roadblocks along the Way?
- To learn about those to whom Mr. Fox turns for advice, go to Chapter Nine: Who Is in Your PLN?

PRINCIPAL MARTINEZ

Our high school leader, Ms. Martinez, had recently had a few teachers question her coaching. They wondered how it was going to affect their evaluations. After visiting classrooms with her coach (in this case, me, in the above math example) and discussing the issue, Ms. Martinez decides it's time for a frank conversation with her staff. Rather than speak to over one hundred teachers in a faculty meeting, Ms. Martinez decides she will visit each department. In order to continue to build the capacity of her AP's, Ms. Martinez will take with her the AP who oversees each department for each meeting.

In each meeting, Ms. Martinez explains the same basic concept. First, she reminds her staff that she is a lifelong learner and that she is constantly striving to be a better leader for them and their students. She explains that she has been working with a coach to enhance her skills and shares what an amazing learning experience it has been for her. Next she shares that since one of her passions is instructional leadership and one of her primary responsibilities is to ensure that students are learning and achieving, she and the AP's have been working on a variety of ways to visit classrooms more frequently and to provide relevant feedback to teachers. She asks a few teachers if they would be willing to share their experience with her coaching conversations with them. Because Ms. Martinez made a point to focus on one teacher in each department for her coaching, she has at least one volunteer in every meeting. When the staff hears one of their colleagues express that they valued the one-to-one time with the boss and the specific feedback and ensuing conversation, some of them become much less tense about the new observation schedules.

After meeting with each department, Ms. Martinez schedules a follow-up meeting with her site union representatives. She wants a chance to debrief with them and to see if they have any feedback to share with her. During that meeting, Ms. Martinez hears that while many teachers understand and support the additional coaching attempts, there are some who are concerned about retaliation and evaluation ramifications. When Ms. Martinez presses the reps to be explicit about whom and what situations to which they are referring, she is not given specifics. Ms. Martinez reiterates that their administrative team's coaching philosophy is grounded in a strength-based approach and that they are all working to help all teachers continue to improve their practice in order to better serve all students. If she, or any AP, had concerns about an individual teacher's performance, that would be made clear in a conversation. If anything was leading towards a negative evaluation, the teacher would know and understand that ahead of time, and they would be welcome to invite a union rep to attend any evaluation meetings.

After her meeting with the union reps, Ms. Martinez debriefs with her AP's. As a group, they feel the coaching message was well-received by most of their staff. They plan to continue to build relationships with key teacher leaders and to start asking other teachers how they prefer to receive feedback.

- To learn about Ms. Martinez's next steps to build teacher leadership, go to Chapter Four: What Is the Role of a Teacher Leader as an Instructional Coach?

Chapter Three
WHAT IS THE ROLE OF AN ADMINISTRATOR AS INSTRUCTIONAL LEADER AND COACH?

Leadership is not about building trust so that the hard work of improvement can happen later. It is about tackling the work in ways that build trust through learning and making progress together.

–VIVIANE ROBINSON, Student-Centered Leadership

Today's school administrators wear many hats. Since my first days in administration (many years ago), there has been much talk about the principal as the lead learner, the instructional leader of a school. As I support new leaders today, however, I've noticed that many struggle to fit in the role of instructional leader—and may ignore the role of coach completely. These shortcomings typically stem from the reality that it is challenging to balance all the elements of a complex job (see the time management chapter for some tips on this later) and from a fear that they don't know enough to coach teachers.

If you are an administrator who wants teachers to see you as an instructional coach, start by defining your coaching work and sharing your definition transparently with your teachers. We will talk more about designing your own coaching model in a later chapter. For now, take a moment to reflect on this question, as it will be one of the first things your teachers will need to know: *How will your instructional coaching differ from evaluation?*

You need to be able to answer the question clearly for your teachers. No matter what you say, if they don't trust you, they won't believe that your "coaching" will be any different from an evaluation.

Building trusting relationships takes time. It can take months or even years for a teacher to trust a new administrator. Many teachers have worked with anywhere from one to twenty administrators (especially if you include vice/assistant principals) throughout their careers. Often they have been at a school longer than anyone on the administrative team, so their skepticism or uncertainty about a new administrator isn't unexpected or unreasonable. Building trust starts with the administrator, which is why I encourage all administrators to be visible on campus, in classrooms, and at school events—especially if they are new to a school.

No matter how long you've been at your school, make time to meet new colleagues. Get to know your teachers by asking about their work and their personal lives. And always make a point to greet everyone by name.

Active listening will help you in this endeavor of building relationships. Do a lot more listening than talking as you get to know others. When people truly feel heard, they feel closer to the people who took time to listen to them. Over time, your efforts will lead to trust. Active listening will also help you in your role as an instructional coach.

> *When people truly feel heard, they feel closer to the people who took time to listen to them.*

As a new principal, I immediately began visiting classrooms and leaving little notes, celebrating something I saw the teacher doing well for students and posing what I thought was a reflective question (more on this in a later chapter). I was surprised when my teachers began freaking out about my little notes and asking everyone else before finally asking me, "What are you looking for?" At first, I didn't understand their concern or confusion. I was looking for good teaching, of course!

Then I realized that I had not shared my definition of good teaching; in fact, I hadn't even clearly defined it for myself or provided guidance on how to make good teaching a measurable goal. I quickly backtracked and began to have instructional conversations with teachers, so we could craft a common understanding of some big instructional buzz words, such as *student engagement, wait time*, and *checking for understanding*. This took time, and I realized teachers would need to visit one another's classrooms to find and agree upon a common language. Our lesson studies really helped us build this language—live—while we were lesson planning and delivering lessons together. (You'll learn more about lesson studies in Chapter Eight.)

As a staff, we determined which instructional strategies were going to help our students learn and make progress. We did this through district- and site-based professional development. We also read and used research, professional articles, and books as our references for high-leverage strategies that would support the students we served. As we began to practice those strategies together, I was able to become an administrator who provided instructional coaching for the staff in a focused way.

LEAD BY WALKING AROUND

Every new school year, new leadership position and interaction provides us with the opportunity to build or strengthen relationships with individual staff members and students in our schools. The time to step away from your office and lead by walking around is now.

During my time as a site leader, I made a point to visit each teacher's classroom during the opening setup days before students returned to school. While these visits took me out of the office and away from the nonstop stream of emails and phone calls that would await my return, they were a powerful way for me to build new relationships or renew past relationships with each staff member. Not only could I check in with people about their summer and their family, I was also able to check out their room setup and offer my support physically, emotionally, or professionally. These short personal visits helped me learn more about my staff members as individuals and as members of our learning community.

I visited each classroom again after every school break. These visits did not have the same purpose as my instructional visits, which were to provide evidence-based feedback to individual teachers or to the staff about student learning and instructional practices based on our current learning focus. Post-vacation visits were all about maintaining relationships. I stopped in to greet teachers and students and welcome them back. I learned about their time away from school, their families, and their hobbies. In other words, I got to know them all just a little bit better.

I also made sure to regularly visit our school's custodians, cafeteria staff, instructional assistants, and clerical staff. Leaders need to build and maintain relationships with all staff members. This practice helps build a positive culture. As you model the importance of building relationships, your staff members do the same, building positive relationships with students. In one school, I noticed that our cafeteria staff members were very terse and unfriendly with students during the lunch rush. I began to spend my time during lunch supervision right near the lunch lines, interacting with students and staff, making sure I had a big smile on my face the entire time. As I modeled this behavior, I noticed the cafeteria staff began to do the same. Slowly, I saw more smiles and less curtness when the staff interacted with students buying lunch. While this may seem like a small change, this is where culture and climate come together on a school campus and can make a huge difference in your students feeling welcome and safe.

Working as a central-office leader, I consider it even more important to lead by walking around, to be visible at schools, in classrooms, and at events. I visit schools today to coach our leaders. I don't know many of the teachers because I came to the school district in this role not having worked at any of our sites.

When the administrative leaders and I go into classrooms to observe student learning and instructional practices, I often meet teachers for the first time. I always follow up my visits with a personal email to the teachers, copying the team who was with us on the visit, to thank them for the work they do and to share something I appreciated in their room that was positively affecting student learning. This is one small way for me to build connections in a large district with thousands of staff members. As I do this, I am also modeling for the site leaders some ways they can build and maintain relationships with their staff.

The time you invest in relationships leads to deeper trust, which can enhance your team, school, or system's culture. This time will provide you a bridge to becoming an instructional leadership coach.

ARE YOU COACHING OR EVALUATING?

Differentiating between your coaching and your evaluation will be important. As a site leader, our evaluation procedures were outlined in our collective bargaining agreements with our unions. I was able to follow those procedures and outline the evaluation process at the beginning of each school year with all teachers being evaluated. The process began with teachers writing their own professional goals for the year and then meeting with me to review and agree upon those goals. As a principal, I would then schedule two formal observations as part of my evaluation of a teacher. Teachers knew these were different from my informal observations because (1) they were always pre-scheduled on an agreed-upon date and time, (2) I required a written lesson plan ahead of time, (3) I would stay through an entire lesson (usually about an hour or a full class period), and (4) we scheduled a formal debriefing meeting after the observation.

In contrast, my informal observations were for coaching purposes. These unannounced visits, often ten to twenty minutes long, were followed up by written or in-person feedback provided when we were able to be together to discuss it.

We educators take our work seriously and want to do our jobs well. We get up every day determined to do the best we can for the students or staff we serve. Done well, evaluations can help us achieve that goal. Unfortunately, most educators have experienced evaluations that weren't very meaningful to our professional growth. This has certainly been true in my career. In my first two years of teaching, I never had an administrator enter my room. Around March, when I knew I was moving from Virginia to California and that I would need a letter of recommendation from an administrator, I begged my assistant principal to come visit my room, so he could have something to write about in a letter for me. My final evaluation from him consisted of a list of instructional strategies and a box checked "satisfactory" next to each one. He offered no other additional notes or suggestions. I knew as a new teacher that I still had lots to learn, but I wasn't going to learn it through my evaluation process.

A colleague of mine at another school never saw her administrator all year. On the day evaluations were due, her principal walked into her room and asked her to sign the evaluation he had completed on her that year. It was based on nothing because they had never met, never established goals, and had never conducted an observation or even a conversation. His "evaluation" included a list of six statements based on the California Standards for the Teacher Profession (CSTPs), with a space for the administrator to check a box that my friend was meeting or not meeting each standard. While the CSTPs are a great resource for teachers, the way we often see them used as a final evaluation have little impact on teaching or learning. In California, the CSTPs drive how to support new teachers through the induction process and can support the ongoing professional growth of all teachers if they are used to setting personal goals and to tracking progress over time. Your state may not have common standards for teachers, but you do have an evaluation process. California also has standards for educational leaders, which are modeled after the national standards for leaders.

Experiences like these make many educators feel that the evaluation process does nothing to help them grow as professionals. Because of this and because many evaluation procedures are driven by clear and non-negotiable language in collective bargaining agreements, administrators must distinguish between evaluation and instructional coaching.

Instructional coaching should be an ongoing, flexible process that is driven by the teacher's individual needs and built and fortified by trust. Coaching should feel less formal than evaluation and should take place in a variety of settings, including side-by-side coaching inside a classroom, conversations during passing periods, and sit-down meetings held after class. As an educator, evaluations will also play a role in your career whether you are on the receiving end or completing them to evaluate others. To make evaluations effective, the purpose, expectations, and feedback must be clear.

CHOOSE THE COACH ADVENTURE

If you have just arrived from Chapter One and are curious about how Mr. Fox's Professional Development day goes, keep reading.

If you have just arrived from Chapter Three, where Ms. Martinez had explained to her staff the importance of her role as an instructional coach, you can skip down to continue the story.

PRINCIPAL FOX

When we left Principal Fox, our elementary colleague was excited about the professional development day he had co-planned with a group of teacher leaders.

The PD went very well, and during the discussions that day, the staff agreed that

Instructional coaching should be an ongoing, flexible process that is driven by the teacher's individual needs and built and fortified by trust.

the school's focus should be around two key areas: supporting academic language for English Learners and increasing parent engagement. The feedback from teachers after the PD was very positive:

- We appreciated hearing from our colleagues leading sessions today!
- Thank you for the time to collaborate!
- I feel like I know what our focus is more than ever before.

The teachers also raised some important questions throughout the learning day:

- How can we get feedback on our work?
- How can we make sure we don't get sidetracked with a million new ideas again?
- How can we share what is going well in our classes and across the site?

Principal Fox took some time to reflect after the PD session. He was pleased that the day had gone well and that the feedback from the staff was positive. He felt confident that the two focus areas selected by the staff were aligned with what they should be doing, though he realized that his site plan and some of his previous goals were not yet aligned to this work. He knew he would need to meet with his School Site Council (SSC) to revise the site plan based on their renewed focus. Principal Fox also wanted to meet with his Parent-Teacher Association (PTA) president to talk about how he could partner with the PTA to support the goal of increasing parent engagement at the school. He would also need to work with his teacher leadership team to discuss what resources and supports they could offer staff around these two initiatives.

Mr. Fox had heard his teachers' requests for feedback on their work; he knew it was time to begin visiting their rooms and observing with a coaching lens. He clarified for his staff how and when this would begin and how this role of an instructional coach would look different from his evaluator or manager role.

Mr. Fox followed through and began to visit classrooms, only to hit a snag: He wasn't sure what to do or how to actually coach his teachers. He felt like he was visiting rooms randomly and without a clear focus. His teachers wondered how long this would continue. Would he soon return to his office, only to be seen at meetings or for discipline issues? At the same time, Mr. Fox felt like he was being pulled in all directions, and he was struggling to get his work done every day.

- If you want to know more about Mr. Fox's next coaching steps, go to Chapter Six: What Does Coaching Look Like?
- If you want to see how Mr. Fox begins to work on his calendar, go to Chapter Eleven: What Do Coaches Need to Know about Time Management?

PRINCIPAL MARTINEZ

Martinez had begun to visit classrooms regularly, providing teachers with feedback on what was going well for students and what strengths she observed in instruction. Some of her more vocal teacher leaders soon came to her asking if her feedback was going to be on their evaluations. Ms. Martinez quickly called up her coach for support. Her coach helped her understand the importance of distinguishing between her informal observations and feedback versus her formal evaluations, which followed the prescribed district procedures. After getting clarity by talking with her coach, Principal Martinez explained the difference to her staff, but she realized that her staff still wasn't clear on what instructional coaching was all about. At the same time, Ms. Martinez's coach helped her see that she needed to bring her leadership team, her assistant principals, along with her on her own coaching adventure.

- To learn about coaching skills alongside Ms. Martinez, go to Chapter Two: What Are Instructional Leadership Coaching Skills?
- To learn more about how Ms. Martinez approached coaching, go to Chapter Six: What Does Coaching Look Like?

Chapter Four
WHAT IS THE ROLE OF A TEACHER LEADER AS AN INSTRUCTIONAL COACH?

Every person who enters the field of education has both an opportunity and an obligation to be a leader.

−RICHARD DUFOUR AND ROBERT J. MARZANO,
Leaders of Learning: How District, School, and Classroom
Leaders Improve Student Achievement

Teacher leaders play an important role on a campus. First and foremost, teachers demonstrate leadership in their own classrooms every day. Teachers model leadership for our students. Teacher leaders facilitate professional learning community (PLC) meetings and lesson studies. They provide instructional coaching and feedback to peers, formally and informally. They also support a school's instructional focus through their team leadership. In some schools, teacher leaders participate in learning walks and peer observations, visiting other classrooms on their own or with a team of people observing for a specific focus. But what coaching training do teacher leaders receive?

In most schools, a teacher is volunteered, "voluntold" (credit to my former boss who uses this strategy to build capacity), recruited, or appointed to a leadership position without any formal support. There is no university coursework or certification process for most teacher leaders, though universities are exploring options for this today. Each district defines its own formal teacher leadership positions, but each principal's actions determine the level of leadership a teacher is expected to take or respected for taking.

When I was a new principal, I was not good at building teacher leadership capacity; in fact, when I first became a principal, this idea wasn't even on my radar. I did not have a clue that it was my responsibility to help develop teacher leadership in my staff. Fast-forward to my work as a district-level administrator, and I can now see the error of my ways. Teacher leaders are the backbone of any long lasting initiative.

Yes, we need site principals to build trust, set the vision, and help people see the purpose of any new initiative. But after the initial cheerleading and encouragement, the hands-on work falls to teachers—the people with boots on the ground, sleeves rolled up, doing the work every day with students.

When they are knee-deep in a stressful, new learning situation, teachers will more often look to their peers than to their administrators. To seek support, teachers will call their department chair, their PLC leader, their site technology support, or the colleague who teaches next door.

Administrators often encourage strong teachers, those with natural leadership abilities, to become administrators. That is often the only leadership option for many teachers. But not all teachers want to leave their classroom full time, and we shouldn't want all strong teacher leaders to leave teaching positions.

So what are we doing, as leaders and coaches, to build the capacity of the teacher leaders within our system? Our goals should be to enhance the leadership skills of teachers currently serving in some teacher-leadership capacity and to develop leadership skills in teachers not yet serving in such a role.

My principal and mentor developed my leadership as a teacher by visiting my classroom frequently, providing me evidence-based feedback on what I was doing that positively impacted my students, then providing me opportunities to share my work with my peers.

Before I had the title of peer coach, I was coaching my peers. I did this in staff meetings when I modeled a strategy that had worked well for my students. I did this in my PLC when I was encouraged to share my ideas and the evidence of success from my classroom.

One of the scariest times I acted as a peer coach was when my principal made me a demonstration-classroom teacher. My classroom became a room where teachers from my own school, from other schools in our large, urban district, or even from other states and countries could visit to learn. I once had twenty-five Chinese educators in my room—along with a team of district leaders—observing my lesson! The demonstration classroom (or "lab site," as it was called) was open for visitors any time. If my principal wanted a particular teacher to see a specific skill in action, she would let me know, so we could arrange a scheduled observation with that purpose. Sometimes the principal would bring teachers in with her, so she could side-by-side coach them as they watched me teach. Other times teachers would roam in on their own, staying as long as it was relevant for their learning. If they had questions or wanted to talk, they would find me to discuss their observations.

The power of a demonstration classroom is that the learning is facilitated by teachers for teachers. Instead of reading about an instructional strategy, a teacher can see it in action with real students. When a teacher feels like their students can't or won't do something, they can see a model of students just like theirs working on the challenging skill, task, or idea. This is the potential of teacher leadership coaching.

Just like with administrators who work as instructional coaches, teacher leaders need knowledge of adult learning theory, an understanding of coaching models, clarity on educational pedagogy and student learning, and the ability to build trusting relationships with colleagues.

STEPPING INTO A TEACHER LEADER ROLE

If you are a teacher leader stepping into an instructional coach role, I encourage you to seek clarity in these areas from your principal. What are your site's instructional goals? How will your coaching support the site's goals? Once you have a clear understanding of your role, you need to ensure that your colleagues understand your role and how you can support them. If you are new to a school, you need to take the time to build positive relationships, so teachers can trust you. If you have been teaching at your school and have transitioned into a coaching role, part of your responsibility is helping your colleagues understand that transition. This requires a different kind of relationship building so that your peers trust you in your new role.

Your peers will need to know that you are not reporting everything they share with you to the principal. They need to trust that your coaching is about helping them be the best they can be and not changing them based on what the principal wants or expects. Nor is it about making them into clones of you.

There is power in teachers seeking out coaching from their peers. When teachers serve in the role of an instructional leadership coach, they bring with them their experience as a teacher. They are often still part-time teachers or very recently removed from being full-time teachers. Teachers respect coaching when it is relevant to their context and shared by someone who has real and recent experience teaching students.

As a teacher leader serving as a coach, whether full or part time, it's important that you develop open communication between you and the teachers you serve. Here are some thoughts to consider:
- How will teachers request your coaching support?
- In what areas are you able to provide coaching and support?
- What does your coaching look like? Is it a one-time event or a cycle? (See Chapter Six for more on this.)
- What will your principal know about the coaching? Are your coaching conversations confidential?
- Is the coaching individual, or can a PLC be involved together?

If you are a teacher leader interested in stepping into a coaching role but don't have a formal title, there are small steps you can begin to take:

Open your classroom for others to come observe you, asking for feedback from your administrators and your peers. The #ObserveMe movement created by Robert Kaplinsky provides a great model for a way you can seek feedback on your instruction from anyone who enters your classroom. (https://robertkaplinsky.com/observeme).

Speak to your school or district administrators about your own instructional expertise. You can offer to facilitate professional development workshops on site or for district-wide events. You can also apply to present at state or national conferences. Your peers and administrators will see you as a leader if you step into this new role, as your passion will shine through when you are sharing something you consider your strength.

Volunteer to be observed and to observe others during Learning Walks or Instructional Rounds or any other forms of peer observations. Not only will this help you gain clarity on your site's goals, but you will also have a deeper understanding of what teaching looks like across your site. One of the biggest shocks a teacher leader can have is the first time they step into a peer's classroom whose teaching is nothing like they might have imagined. Hearing someone discuss their practice during a PLC can be very different from seeing them live in action in front of students. More on this in Chapter Twelve about the challenges coaches face.

Stay current on educational research. I keep a revolving list of professional books to read and a list of books and blogs I can recommend to others. If your district has 1:1 technology devices for students, you'd better know how to integrate technology effectively into your classroom practice. Being a teacher leader on a campus can feel isolating, so using social media can help (more on this in Chapter Nine).

HOW TO SUPPORT TEACHER LEADERS

As a district leader, I have found a few ways to support teacher leadership development across our district. One way was to connect with local teachers who were active on Twitter and recruit them to help me build a monthly district Twitter chat. I also found a core group of teachers and leaders who would host an Edcamp with me. Together we created Edcamp619.

During this past school year, due to some specific funding, I was able to create a Teacher Leadership Academy along with a colleague. This was designed to support teachers who wanted more leadership skills but weren't interested in stepping into administrative positions. The Academy met monthly for a two-hour evening meeting where we discussed elements of teacher leadership, such as our core values, being on a team, dealing with difficult people, working through conflicts, and facilitating meetings. The feedback we received from the teacher leaders who attended was overwhelmingly positive. They stay in touch, supporting one another through cross-site visits, Twitter chats, emails, and personal meetups. I love seeing their positive, uplifting Tweets encouraging one another!

Moving forward, you might be stepping into a specific coaching role, or you might be stepping out of your comfort zone as a teacher leader. No matter your position or title, this is your opportunity to help your peers strengthen their skills and knowledge on behalf of students. Lean into your own strengths and what has been successful in your own classroom with your students. Find peers and mentors who will support your learning during this time whether they are your own site principal or a friend you've met through your Professional Learning Network (PLN). Share your thoughts, successes, and questions with our community using the #CoachADV hashtag.

CHOOSE THE COACH ADVENTURE

If you have just arrived from Chapter One and are curious about how Mr. Fox worked to build teacher leadership capacity or you've arrived from Chapter Seven where Mr. Fox was learning how to listen as a coach, continue reading.

If you've just arrived from Chapter Eleven where Ms. Martinez was struggling to engage teachers in coaching or you've arrived from Chapter Two where Ms. Martinez and her team want to build teacher leadership, skip down to continue your journey with Principal Martinez.

PRINCIPAL FOX

Mr. Fox was beyond impressed by the way his teachers co-planned and co-facilitated the professional development day. He wanted to capitalize on this success and tap into his teachers' strengths as he began to build his own instructional coaching capabilities.

As he led his leadership team through a debrief about the PD day, he took time to ask them each what they felt their instructional strengths were. He explained that he wanted to find different ways to highlight their strengths for the benefit of the entire staff and to ultimately make a greater impact on students.

At first, the teachers seemed hesitant to name their strengths, offering self-deprecating answers. One teacher, though, finally shared that she felt she was good at being positive with her students and that she was working on her feedback techniques. Her response helped others to open up. His next question was much easier for his leadership team members to answer: "What goals are you working on?" Before ending the meeting, everyone on the team agreed to try the #ObserveMe challenge in their own classrooms as a way to model their own goal setting with their peers.

After the meeting, one shy teacher came up to speak to Mr. Fox privately. She admitted that she didn't want to brag in front of her peers but that she felt confident in her abilities to engage students, especially in math. Mr. Fox agreed with her, citing something he had recently observed in her room. Mr. Fox asked the teacher if she would consider opening up her room during math time, so her peers could observe her engagement strategies. While he didn't yet know to call this a demonstration classroom, Mr. Fox was beginning to understand the value in building his teachers' capacity to strengthen staff professional growth.

- To learn how Mr. Fox uses his teacher leadership skills to build a culture of learning with his staff, go to Chapter Eight: How Can Lesson Study Support Coaching?
- To learn how Mr. Fox builds his coaching plan, go to Chapter Five: What Is a Coaching Theory of Action?

PRINCIPAL MARTINEZ

Teacher engagement in informal observation and coaching process had been a struggle for Principal Martinez. During their leadership team meeting, Ms. Martinez asked her team to think about one teacher in their departments who had the potential to be a teacher leader. She explained that this person didn't have to be the official department or grade level or PLC chair but could simply be a teacher who made positive connections with students and staff, who excelled in some instructional strategies, whose students loved and respected her or him, or who had a lot of knowledge to share with others. Ms. Martinez and her team brainstormed how they could each work with their individual teachers to build their teacher leadership capacity. The team agreed to the following:

- Make time to observe this teacher frequently and provide feedback.
- Make time to have personal conversations with this teacher, sharing feedback and getting to know this teacher's goals and aspirations.
- Find a way to encourage this teacher to take on a leadership role through one of the following things:
  » Speak out more in PLC, department, or staff meetings by sharing a strong instructional strategy that was successful with students.
  » Volunteer to serve on a site committee that would benefit from his or her expertise.
  » Visit a peer to provide feedback on the site focus areas.
  » Invite a peer to visit him or her to provide feedback on a specific area of focus.
  » Start an #ObserveMe challenge.
  » Share instructional successes via Twitter, using the school's hashtag.

After a month, the team revisited their teacher leadership discussion, sharing what successes and challenges they had experienced in the previous month. Two of the AP's felt they had developed a close bond with their chosen teachers, and they had evidence of their teachers stepping into a positive leadership role on campus. One assistant principal had struggled with his teacher. Ms. Martinez realized this assistant principal needed more direct support from her, as his instructional leadership still needed work as well. She decided that in her one-on-one time with him, she would model some conversations she'd had with teacher leaders around campus. She would also involve this assistant principal in her planning for their site instructional leadership team meetings.

The team agreed to continue to work to build the capacity of their teacher leader and to help that teacher leader bring in other teachers to their good work. In a large high school, this work felt like dropping a pebble into the ocean at first, but as word spread, a few departments really began to see noticeable changes. The ripples were small at first: The English department began to host a monthly Twitter chat, inviting other staff members to participate. In the science department, the #ObserveMe challenge really took off, and soon the science teachers were regularly observing one another.

As Ms. Martinez watched teacher leadership develop through the coaching by her team, she realized it was time to channel their efforts into a specific instructional focus that would benefit students, especially if she wanted these ripples to create a wave of change.

- To read about her next steps with one department at Learning for All High School, go to Chapter Eight: How Can Lesson Study Support Coaching?
- To read about how Ms. Martinez brings teachers into professional development through observations, go to Chapter Ten: How Do Coaches Facilitate Collaborative Professional Learning?

Part II
Building Instructional Capacity through Coaching

We've talked about leadership and coaching in general as well as the skill set an instructional coach needs. Now it's time to talk about why coaching is important and how you can build instructional capacity. For any leader who wants to improve student learning, the starting point is with the teachers in the classroom.

I'm sure many of you, like me, have had leaders who wanted to help you succeed but didn't have the training they needed or a plan. So they told you what to do, handed you a book or a guide they expected you to follow, then left you alone in your room to do whatever you wanted. Unfortunately, this haphazard method leaves our students' learning and classroom experiences up to chance.

Intentional coaching can build the instructional capacity of teachers. Whether that coaching comes from administrators or other teachers, when the focus is on helping educators positively impact students, everyone wins.

For any leader who wants to improve student learning, the starting point is with the teachers in the classroom.

Chapter Five
WHAT IS A COACHING THEORY OF ACTION?

Draw a different frame around the same set of circumstances and new pathways come into view.
—ROSAMUND STONE ZANDER AND
BENJAMIN ZANDER, The Art of Possibility

Your personal coaching theory of action, which is the foundation of the coaching model we discussed in Part I, will guide your work as a leader and a coach. But what is a coaching theory of action? A coaching theory of action sets out to describe your purpose. Why are you a coach? What do you believe in that drives your coaching work? In order to positively impact the teaching practice of others, you must define what you want to do as a coach and why.

IDENTIFY YOUR CORE VALUES

The first step in designing your own coaching theory of action is to identify your core values. What drives you to do the work you do? What are you most passionate about within that work? We must know ourselves first. This is our foundation. Then we need to recognize that each and every person with whom we work operates from their own core values, none of which will be identical to our own.

As a young teacher, a teacher leader, and even an assistant principal and principal, no one ever asked me what my core values were. It wasn't until I began to read the work of Elena Aguilar and to study coaching and leadership at deeper levels that I stopped to define my own core values. Through a number of reflective processes, I currently define my core values as:

- Trust
- Equity
- Making a Difference
- Empathy

I am focused on my core values as a leader, an educator, a coach, and a mentor. My core values drive me to do more, to seek support, and to coach in order to build capacity.

Trust is a non-negotiable in my life. This would not have been on my list twenty years ago, but I was a younger, more naive educator twenty years ago who didn't know how critical trust was. The more I work with new leaders, the more I emphasize the importance of taking time to build authentic relationships to develop trust. Without trust, initiatives will not have long lasting success, and staff and students will suffer. When a new administrator tries to make big changes early on in a new role, the staff may not yet trust that the administrator is doing something that will benefit the school—and the initiative may struggle or fail. But when trust is built over time by leaders who are consistent with doing what they say they will do—following up, communicating honestly, and listening to the needs of others—positive strides can be made.

Trust must be earned. It must also be protected. Trust can easily be broken if a staff member feels the leader acted in his or her best interest instead of in the best interest of the students, staff, and community. Trust truly does make or break a leader.

Equity might not have made it to a list of my core values twenty years ago either. It took all the years I have taught, coached, and served in neighborhoods where the average income was well below the poverty level to see the critical needs in our society. I was also learning about all the inequities in education and discovering the importance of social justice leadership. Equality is about everyone getting the same thing at the same time. Equity is everyone getting what they need when they need it. There are students who enter our schools in kindergarten who are already behind due to circumstances beyond their control. They have unearned disadvantages that put them behind students who grow up with unearned advantages before they've even started school. When I advocate for equity, I hope to provide a voice for the students and families in our communities who have been marginalized and disregarded or who are unable to speak for themselves.

I am also driven by the desire to make a difference on behalf of students, teachers, staff, and other leaders. In my coaching and leading, I want to make a difference in the lives of other educators, so they impact students. Making a difference is why I am here. I became a teacher to make a difference in the lives of my students. I became a coach and an administrator to make a difference in the lives of educators and to indirectly impact more students.

Empathy became a core value after years of coaching others. It's easy to jump to the wrong conclusion when coaching a colleague. *Why would she do that activity? Why didn't he plan for the students to talk before they wrote? What was she thinking? I would have done something different.* But coaching is not about telling people what to do or creating copycat versions of ourselves. Coaching is about helping people to get better at their craft

> **When the focus is on helping educators positively impact students, everyone wins.**

in their own way. I love how George Couros, author of *The Innovator's Mindset*, talks about this: "Effective leadership in education is not about moving everyone from one standardized point to the next but moving individuals from their point 'A' to their point 'B.'" Those points are not the same for each educator. In order to do this, a coach needs to presume positive intentions and empathize with her colleagues.

In a workshop where I was asked to define, in one tweet, why I lead (140 characters only—I miss this shorter tweet requirement!), I wrote: *To create equitable learning environments where student and adult learners thrive. #whyIlead*

Take some time to identify your core values. What drives you as an instructional leader and coach? Can you capture #WhyICoach or #WhyILead in one tweet-worthy statement? If so, please share with our community, using the hashtag #CoachADV.

ARTICULATE YOUR COACHING BELIEFS

Elena Aguilar writes in *The Art of Coaching*, "We do not really see through our eyes or hear through our ears, but through our beliefs." The next step in developing your coaching theory of action is to articulate your coaching beliefs. Your coaching beliefs are statements that drive your work as a coach. They are the elements of a coaching relationship and a structure that is important to you. Coaching beliefs determine the ways in which you approach colleagues for coaching conversations.

Here are my coaching beliefs:

- **Coach from a place of strengths.** We all have strengths, and the best way for me to coach is to start from an individual's strengths. People are often more willing to hear suggestions and take new actions if a coaching conversation begins by acknowledging the hard work, dedication, and positive elements already in place.
- **Voice and choice matter.** We each learn and grow when we have a say in our learning. When I coach, I work hard to listen and to provide an opportunity for teachers to have a voice about their teaching. I also work to provide choice; there is not just one way to coach, teach, or do something. The more voice and choice an individual has, the more empowered he or she is to make a positive change.
- **All must mean all.** All students can learn, all teachers can grow, all leaders can be coaches; anything is possible when we all come together as a community. This means that I coach, learn, and collaborate with a positive belief in those I work with and for. This also means that I have to challenge statements and actions that go against a belief in the success of all.
- **We are lifelong learners.** All of my work is grounded in the belief that we are all lifelong learners. I do not believe that I have all the answers, but I am committed to learning new

information whenever I can. I strive to model the seeking and cultivating of new learning. Coaches are leaders on a school site and at the district level, and I believe that a coach can demonstrate true lifelong learning in thoughts and actions. This is why my standard email signoff is "Always learning, Amy."

- **Trust matters.** Change does not occur without a trusting relationship present. As a coach I believe in the teachers with whom I work, and I dedicate time to develop trust. Trust comes from mutual respect, following through on promises, demonstrating competency, and a willingness to be open, honest, and imperfect together.
- **Walk the walk and talk the talk.** I am a coach who is not afraid to get my hands dirty with model lessons, collaborative planning sessions, shared frustrations, shared successes, and more. Coaches are only coaches if they walk the walk MORE than they talk the talk!
- **There is not just one "right" answer.** Coaching is about a process, a journey, and not one specific destination; in addition, coaching is not about getting educators to my personal belief, but to support them on their journey to be their best self. As a coach, I work to help others find their best processes along this journey.

I encourage you to write down your coaching beliefs and make them public. This is the second step in building your coaching theory of action. Here are some questions to consider that can help you develop your coaching beliefs:

- When have you received advice that you appreciated? How was that advice given?
- If you were struggling, how would you want others to support you?
- What is your philosophy on learning?
- In what ways have you expanded your knowledge of instructional practices in the past?
- How do you share your learning with others?
- How do you approach colleagues to have a difficult conversation?

DETERMINE THE RELATIONSHIP BETWEEN COACHING AND DESIRED OUTCOMES

The third step towards your coaching theory of action is to determine the relationship between coaching and your desired outcome. The outcome is often better student learning, but any other challenge (e.g., school culture) could be the focus of your coaching.

My core value of equity has driven me to become a social justice leader focused on the achievement and opportunity gaps between different groups of students in our educational systems. I am aware of the realities that many of our students face before they even walk through our school doors. Some students begin their educational careers already behind their peers due to unearned disadvantages they were born with or born into—circumstances over which they have little to no control. These factors highlight the importance of a sound instructional program that differentiates support based on an individual student's learning needs.

CREATE STRUCTURES TO SUPPORT INSTRUCTIONAL LEADERSHIP COACHING

Because I believe so strongly that every student can learn when given the support he or she needs, I know how important it is to invest in improving the instructional capacity of teachers. Teachers need support to meet the diverse and challenging learning needs of students who show up in their classrooms every day. Instructional leadership coaching can provide teachers this much-needed support.

The final and often missed step in a coaching plan is to create structures at the school and district level to support instructional leadership coaching. Coaching needs to be defined, and instructional coaches need their own coaches for feedback and growth; for instance, one important structure is to create a coach role with a clear job description. This provides the time, space, and a person who is responsible for coaching others. Another structure would be to provide certain teachers an extra prep period in their schedule, so they can spend that time coaching their peers. At the district level, a supportive structure would be to schedule regular time when site-based coaches come together for their own professional development and support.

MY COACHING THEORY OF ACTION

If you read my coaching theory of action from right to left using if or then statements, you can see how outcomes drive the action:

- If I want to improve student learning, then I need to improve the instructional capacity of teachers.
- If I want to improve the instructional capacity of teachers, then I need to provide instructional leadership coaching.
- If I want to provide instructional leadership coaching, then I need structures (at the site and district level) to support instructional leadership coaching.

What is your coaching theory of action? How will you share your theory of action with your colleagues? Consider the following questions as you begin to craft your theory of action:

- What is your outcome?
- Why is instructional coaching important?
- How will instructional coaching be delivered?
- Who will benefit from your instructional coaching?
- Is your coaching part of a larger system?
- How will you, as the instructional coach, continue to expand your knowledge?

CHOOSE THE COACH ADVENTURE

If you have just arrived from Chapter Six and are curious about Mr. Fox's coaching beliefs, keep reading.

If you've just arrived from the Introduction or Chapter Six and are curious about how Ms. Martinez will develop a coaching system, skip down to continue her story.

PRINCIPAL FOX

Mr. Fox has begun to work with his teacher leadership team to build their capacity and models of good instruction with their peers. He has also begun to visit classrooms to provide feedback, though both he and his teachers are unsure of what his purpose truly is.

Recognizing that he needs to clarify his vision for coaching, Principal Martinez takes time to reflect on his core values and his coaching beliefs. He thinks that his values include compassion, family, and pride. He wants to be liked, but more than that, he wants to be trusted. He also wants his staff to know he cares about them. He wants his staff to treat one another like family because that is important to him. After some reflection, he realizes that he wants to have pride in his work and his family. When he doesn't feel proud about something, he is hard on himself and doesn't show as much compassion for others.

This leads him to draft the following coaching beliefs:

- I believe that all teachers should feel cared for and like a family.
- I believe that coaching through compassion means that I presume positive intent and speak with kindness in my voice and heart.
- I believe that everyone deserves to be proud of their work; that doesn't mean we have arrived, but we can be proud along the journey.

Coaching through compassion means that I presume positive intent and speak with kindness in my voice and heart.

With his thoughts drafted, he decides to share them at the next staff meeting.

- To learn about how the staff meeting goes, go to Chapter Twelve: How Do Coaches Address Challenges and Roadblocks along the Way?
- To learn about how Mr. Fox puts his coaching beliefs into action, go to Chapter Two: What Are Instructional Leadership Coaching Skills?

PRINCIPAL MARTINEZ

We left Principal Martinez wondering how she could create a more coherent coaching system. Principal Martinez has worked with her own coach over the last few years. She and her coach sit down to discuss what is and is not working about her current coaching model. Principal Martinez lists the following as the strengths of her current coaching work:

- She and her assistant principals are visiting classrooms regularly.
- They are providing feedback to teachers in person and in writing.
- They are collecting data about school-wide trends.

When her coach asked her what the challenges of this current system are, Principal Martinez said the following:

- The feedback given to teachers depends on which administrator delivers it.
- The classroom visits and feedback feel isolated from the rest of the school's work.
- Some teachers seem to appreciate the feedback, while others seem disengaged with the entire process.

Principal Martinez's coach asks her to take a step back and reflect on her own values and beliefs. Her coach gives her a homework assignment to craft her own coaching values and beliefs.

When they come back together, Principal Martinez shares these values and beliefs with her coach. Together they discuss a coaching theory of action for Ms. Martinez that is aligned to the district's coaching plan and the support already provided to her. The coaching theory of action considers the school's focus areas (from their school site plan) and how Principal Martinez will build in additional support for her assistant principals (who are still learning how to be instructional coaches as well).

Once she feels confident in her plan, Ms. Martinez presents her theory of action to her leadership team and asks each of them to craft their own coaching and leading values and beliefs statements. The entire team came back to share their work, and it opened up a new dialogue for them as a team as they worked together to plan a school-wide, coherent plan for instructional coaching. Their plan includes the following:

- A monthly observation schedule that allows each administrator to visit the classrooms and PLCs of the departments they oversee more often than other departments
- A learning walk that the entire leadership team will participate in together once each quarter, so they can calibrate what they are seeing in classrooms and the kind of feedback they are delivering
- A monthly review of the data each leader collects around two school-wide areas (based on their school site plan).
- Monthly visits where the principal will go out to classrooms with one assistant principal for individual coaching conversations

Principal Martinez feels proud of the work she and her team did to create a coherent coaching system for their large comprehensive high school.

- To learn more about how Ms. Martinez and her team implement their coaching plan, go to Chapter Eleven: What Do Coaches Need to Know about Time Management?

Chapter Six
WHAT DOES COACHING LOOK LIKE?

Coaching is unlocking a person's potential to
maximize their growth.

–JOHN WHITMORE

Just as administrators and instructional leaders must take responsibility for building trust with staff, teacher leaders who step into
coaching relationships need to understand the same applies to them
with their peers. That trust is fortified when the peer-to-peer coaching role is clearly defined by the coach, the administrator, and the
district. It's especially important that a clear understanding exists
that the teacher-leader coach is not observing in order to report
back to the principal and that the coach is a peer, not an evaluator.

From my own experience of stepping into a peer coaching role,
I know how important it is that teachers know what the coach's
role is. I am using the term coach throughout this book, but in my
career, I have heard many variations including, but not limited to,
mentor, coach, literacy, math, or content coach, specialist, resource
teacher, staff developer, and instructional coach.

According to dictionary.com, a mentor is a wise and trusted
counselor or teacher.

The same resource has eleven different definitions of a coach,
but none of them relates to the support of teachers. The two closest definitions that we in education have adopted are a person

who trains an athlete or team of athletes or a person who instructs an actor or a singer.

As I reflect on those definitions, I am struck by the differences and the possible ambiguity when this role impacts so many teachers and students. As a system, it is critical that your coaching role be clearly articulated and made public for all to know and understand.

BUILDING RELATIONSHIPS

In any new position, it is critical that you take time to build relationships with your colleagues. Whether you are new to a position or new to a school or district, people need to get to know you in that new role. It takes time to build trust. Without trust, people cannot learn from you, and they are less likely to take risks when it comes to implementing new ideas.

There are many ways to build relationships with people. One of the best ways is to listen. You will read more about listening in the next chapter, but for now, know that you can get to know people by asking simply, "How are you?" or "How's it going?" and then staying quiet as they answer.

People will want to get to know you, so find ways to share little bits about your personal life (having pictures on display of your family, friends, pets, etc., is one way) and your professional experiences without dominating conversations or reciting your resume. Your new colleagues will want to know you are there to be a support to them and that you will be an instructional coach whose goal is to help them meet their own goals. I currently work in a district office with a small team. Though our team is small, our team members have a combined total of seventeen children! (I have zero!) I encouraged our team to create a "kid wall" where they display pictures of their children. Our wall also includes pictures of all our team members' pets. It's fun to walk by and see family members, and the wall is a great way to spark dialogue about what's going on in our lives. (Side note: As of the final editing of this book, I have just transitioned into a new job. One of the first things I noticed in my new department office was a wall of framed photographs. Everyone who works in our department was invited to add their family portrait to the wall. When I saw that, I knew I was in the right place!)

When working with a new coach, teachers are often hesitant to trust him or her until they believe the coach is experienced and well informed. Listening to them, showing them you care, sharing a bit about yourself, then showing them what you know all contribute to building trusting relationships. To let teachers get to know me, one of the first things I did as a newly appointed coach was to create a way to get into each classroom. I did this by asking the teachers if I could come to their room for fifteen minutes to do a read aloud with their students. I explained to the teachers that I wanted to get to know their students. I created a schedule and asked teachers to sign up for a time that was convenient to them.

This brief time in their classrooms served several purposes. It allowed me to introduce myself to the students and see the routines in place in individual classrooms. I could also quickly see who was happy about my new role and welcoming me in, as they were the first to volunteer. I wanted a chance to prove myself to my peers by walking the talk since

> *When teachers can opt-in for the support they desire, they are willing learners in the collaborative relationship.*

that is one of my coaching beliefs. I did that by modeling an interactive read aloud that incorporated metacognition strategies as well as student engagement strategies, two areas of focus for our school at the time. And finally, by planning a mini-lesson where I would teach their students, being in the classroom gave me an opportunity to see what class structures existed for student talk and read alouds in general.

A side note for administrators: I did this same thing as a new principal.

After my initial read aloud mini-lessons, I had a few teachers voluntarily approach me with coaching questions. This was a great way to initiate a coaching relationship with teachers. I encourage new coaches to begin their coaching role on a voluntary basis. If coaching is mandated, it will not be well received. When teachers can opt-in for the support they desire, they are willing learners in the collaborative relationship.

STRENGTH-BASED COACHING

It is also important for new coaches to get to know the strengths of their colleagues. Strength-based coaching begins with a positive relationship highlighting the hard work a teacher is already doing.

The strength-based movement has been around for quite a while. I read the first edition of *Now Discover Your Strengths* by Buckingham and Clifton (after my principal at the time gave it to me as a gift). Since then I have taken the StrengthsFinder quiz as part of a staff book study when I was a principal, with my team of coordinators, in my doctoral program, and in my current role. I was even prompted to go through a strengths-based quiz on the Happify app recently! Every time I take the quiz or discuss strengths with colleagues, I am reminded of the value of starting from a positive place.

How can starting from strengths support coaching? Well, just imagine if every coach entered each conversation from the teacher's strengths. What if teachers knew that coaches (and administrators, for that matter) wanted to discuss their strengths, their positive attributes, and the ways in which they support student learning? We all got into this profession because we care for students and have a love of learning. How might our conversations shift if we remind each other of this in kind, positive ways?

Many leadership classes study the SWOT Analysis to determine the strengths, weaknesses, opportunities, and threats related to a systematic change, initiative, or decision that may impact a school or district. What if we considered elements of this when coaching teachers? What if coaches helped teachers identify their strengths and the opportunities available to enhance their teaching on behalf of the students we serve? How might strength-based coaching enhance your impact? I believe coaching grounded in the teacher's desire to grow as a professional, starting from his or her strengths, develops a solid foundation.

By asking open-ended, non-judgmental, reflective questions (which you will read more about in the next chapter), you can begin each coaching session where the teacher wants to begin. A coach's role, especially when building a new relationship, is to help a teacher articulate his or her own strengths. This conversation can then move into a deeper discussion about the teacher's professional goals, which can lead to coaching work. Coaching with belief in teachers' abilities and high expectations for everyone can transform our schools.

COACHING PLAN

Once a coach has established a relationship and

We all got into this profession because we care for students and have a love of learning. How might our conversations shift if we remind each other of this in kind, positive ways?

begun to approach a teacher through strength-based coaching, it is time to establish a coaching plan. This is a guide for the work, with a commitment from both the teacher and coach, about the outcomes. A coaching plan includes the following:

- **A goal.** What are we working to achieve?
- **An outcome.** How will we know we have achieved our goal?
- **A timeline.** When will we achieve our goal?
- **Roles.** What will the teacher do? What will the coach do?
- **Resources.** What resources will we use?

Sometimes a goal can have a very narrow focus. I once had a teacher, for instance, ask for my support with classroom management in his fourth-period class. The teacher felt like he was having trouble with a few boys in that particular class. He believed the boys were being defiant, and he had tried a number of strategies that worked with previous students, but he wasn't having success and was feeling frustrated. We decided we would work on this for two weeks. We began with me observing his fourth-period

Coaching with belief in teachers' abilities and high expectations for everyone can transform our schools.

class, so I could gather data about the boys and the behavior of the class overall.

Two unexpected outcomes came from this coaching interaction. First, the teacher realized that he didn't know his students that well from a social-emotional lens or an academic lens. The boys in question in his class were each struggling with some personal issues outside of school and were reading well below grade level. This information helped us craft some new strategies for him to try. The second unexpected outcome was that this teacher shared his successes with his colleagues, opening the door for me to build new relationships with a few teachers who, previously, had not been receptive to coaching work with me.

COACHING CYCLE

A coaching plan can often morph into a dedicated coaching cycle. There are various definitions and interpretations of coaching cycles out there. I choose to define coaching cycles for our purpose this way:

1. The teacher and coach establish a mutually agreed-upon focus.
2. The coach employs the gradual release of responsibility over the course of the cycle, beginning with modeling, moving into co-planning and co-teaching and then observing to provide feedback, all around the agreed-upon focus.
3. The coach follows up with observations after the coaching cycle to continue to support, provide positive reinforcement, and offer feedback around the focus.

It is important to select a research-informed focus that will enhance the teacher's instruction and thereby the students' learning.

While teachers often want and need support with individual programs or initiatives, for coaching to have a long-term impact, a coaching focus must be grounded in pedagogy.

A few critical elements must be in place before a coaching cycle like this can be planned or initiated. These elements include the following:

- A trusting relationship between the teacher and coach
- A coach with strong instructional, content, and pedagogical knowledge
- A schedule that allows the coach to spend extended periods of time with a single teacher
- Time for the teacher and coach to debrief and co-plan together before and after each day of the cycle

The element that is most often skipped is the follow-up at the end of a cycle. It is so important to check back in with a teacher after the official cycle has ended to ensure that the teacher has maintained the instructional skill that was taught, modeled, and practiced throughout the cycle. The teacher needs positive reinforcement—if the skill is evident—one, two, and even four weeks after the cycle. Equally important, the teacher needs explicit feedback if the skill is absent during these check-ins. If we believe coaching can impact instruction, we must ensure our cycles include follow-up opportunities to gather data and provide ongoing support for long-term impact.

CHOOSE THE COACH ADVENTURE

If you have just arrived from Chapter Three or Chapter Eleven and are curious about Mr. Fox's initial coaching moves, continue reading.

If you've just arrived from Chapter One or Chapter Three, where Ms. Martinez is defining coaching for her staff to understand, skip down to continue your journey with Principal Martinez.

PRINCIPAL FOX

When we last saw Principal Fox, he was ready to step into the role of an instructional coach but unsure of what to do. He began to implement two things as he visited classrooms on a weekly basis. First, he began to structure his feedback around strength-based coaching. He made sure that he was framing his feedback to teachers around what was going well for students and what strengths he observed in teaching and learning practices. This felt comfortable to him, as it helped him build stronger relationships with his teachers. They quickly began to look forward to his feedback and even began to share his notes with their peers during PLC meetings.

The second idea Mr. Fox implemented was coaching cycles. He approached the fifth-grade lead teacher first. Because this was a grade level Mr. Fox had taught, he was comfortable with the content and structure of the academic work expected of students. The teacher was part of his new leadership team who had helped plan and present at the school professional development day, so the teacher was receptive to seeing some changes take place.

Mr. Fox worked with the teacher to develop a coaching cycle around an area about which the teacher wanted to learn more. The fifth-grade teacher had been struggling to get his students to take initiative with complex math problems, so he wanted to talk about risk-taking and Standard 1 of the CCSS Standards of Mathematical Practice, which asks students to "make sense of problems and persevere in solving them." Together he and Mr. Fox studied the mathematical practice, designed tasks that would require the students to problem solve, and then co-taught lessons around those tasks. Principal Fox encouraged the teacher to consider the academic language supports that would help the English Learners in the class be more successful, as that was one of the school's key initiatives.

Throughout the cycle, the teacher gained confidence in his students' abilities, and Mr. Fox gained confidence in his coaching abilities. He realized he didn't need to be an expert because the value was in the collaborative conversations between the teacher and him about the student learning.

After completing a successful coaching cycle, Mr. Fox read all he could about instructional leadership coaching. He wanted to expand his repertoire before he approached some of his primary-grade teachers.

- To learn about the skills Mr. Fox develops, go to Chapter Two: What Are Instructional Leadership Coaching Skills?

- To learn more about Mr. Fox's coaching beliefs, go to Chapter Five: What Is a Coaching Theory of Action?

PRINCIPAL MARTINEZ

We left our high school principal, Ms. Martinez, ready to step into her instructional coaching role, although her staff was unsure what that was all about. She has been focused on her feedback through a strength-based approach, but she is ready to step into more direct coaching. Ms. Martinez asks one of the English teachers, who also sits on the site leadership team, if she would be willing to work through a coaching cycle with her. Ms. Martinez explains what a coaching cycle is, and the teacher agrees to try it out.

Together they agree to focus on assessment strategies the teacher can use during lessons to check her students' understanding of key concepts. Ms. Martinez observes the class on the first day of the cycle, noting the questions the teacher asks, which students answer, and whether students volunteer or are selected to respond by the teacher. They sit down to debrief after school, and the teacher quickly realizes she had only called on volunteers and that the same three students had dominated that time today. Ms. Martinez and the teacher discuss two options to try the following day: calling on non-volunteers using random selection (By writing each students' name on an index card, the teacher can quickly shuffle through cards to call on a non-volunteer mid-lesson.) and requiring all students to respond via an exit slip at the end of the lesson. Ms. Martinez offers to explain the non-volunteer selection process to the class tomorrow, which the teacher thinks is fine because she isn't sure how to introduce this new idea to her students.

At the end of day two, they meet up to debrief and look through the exit slips together. When Ms. Martinez asks the teacher how she feels about calling on non-volunteers, the teacher shares that she was surprised to hear the voices of a few students who never speak in class. She admits she hadn't realized how little she'd been hearing from them until she had heard their answers today. She agrees to continue to use the index cards, often called equity cards, to select non-volunteers throughout her future lessons. The exit slips are another way for the teacher to "hear" from all students, as they are each required to submit the slip before they leave class. As Ms. Martinez and the teacher review the slips, they agree that there were 20 percent of the students who hadn't fully comprehended the theme of the text they had discussed, while 80 percent were able to articulate it to some degree. They discuss what they might adjust in tomorrow's lesson to help with the confusion of a few.

By the end of the week, Ms. Martinez was feeling good about this first coaching cycle. When she asked the teacher how she thought it went, the teacher said, "Honestly, I thought this was going to be a waste of my time, but I like you and was willing to try something to help you out. This was much more beneficial for me than I expected! I'm happy to now have equity cards to use in my classes, and I can't believe how much more I'm hearing different voices respond throughout lessons. I think using the cards has helped some of my shy students gain confidence to speak as volunteers and non-volunteers. I'm grateful we had this time to work together, and I want to encourage my PLC members to try this with you too."

Ms. Martinez shared this success with her assistant principals and encouraged each of them to try a coaching cycle with one teacher. She knew that her assistant principals had different skill sets, but she wanted to set the expectation that they were all instructional coaches. As they began their cycles, Ms. Martinez recognized that their coaching was still haphazard, and she was looking for more coherence.

One of the assistant principals was much weaker in instruction. After he attempted a coaching cycle, the teacher with whom he worked came to Ms. Martinez to complain.

- To learn more about how Ms. Martinez and her team develop coherence, go to Chapter Five: What Is a Coaching Theory of Action?
- To learn more about how Ms. Martinez addressed the teachers' concerns, go to Chapter Twelve: How Do Coaches Address Challenges and Roadblocks along the Way?

Chapter Seven
WHO IS LISTENING THE MOST?

If the person who talks the most learns the most, who is doing the most learning in your classroom?

–ANONYMOUS

One of the most important roles an instructional leader can take on is that of a coach. When an administrator or teacher steps into a coaching relationship, the goal is to build the instructional capacity of his or her teachers. Although it is essential to know your core values and beliefs as a coach, remember that your role is not to change others' beliefs but to help individuals use their strengths to achieve their own goals.

Administrators are wise to define coaching work separately and clearly for teachers in order to build trust in the process. If teachers perceive an administrator as nothing more than an evaluator "out to get them," the trust has not been established for coaching to occur. If teachers believe that their peer coach reports everything they do back to the principal, trust is also missing. The first step in developing a trusting coaching relationship is for the coach to listen.

Listening is an art that requires active participation and concentration. As a coach, it is important that you take time to listen to teachers. What do your teachers enjoy about their work? What are their professional goals? What hopes do they have for their students' future?

In the past, I have worked with leaders who spent far too much time talking at people without ever listening to what others had to share. In a conversation, if you find yourself listening for a break so you can jump in to say what you've been waiting to say, you need to work on your active listening. Active listening requires you to stay present in the conversation and to listen with the intent of understanding what the speaker is saying.

I have also worked with coaches who felt that the best way to coach or support a teacher was to tell them what to do. This is not coaching and does not require any listening at all. It also has little impact on the relationship or instruction.

The first step in developing a trusting coaching relationship is for the coach to listen.

Listening plays such a critical role in building trusting relationships, especially during times of change. The best coaching and leading takes place when such relationships exist as the foundation of an organization. "Listening skillfully and well to people as they react to change can help them move through their grief reactions and can be a powerful way to build trust in the midst of change," writes Megan Tschannen-Moran in *Trust Matters: Leadership for Successful Schools.*

If I am in a coaching conversation with a teacher, for example, and I hear her say, "I know, but these kids just can't do that," I have learned something important about this teacher's beliefs about our students. I will not interrupt the teacher immediately, but I can make a mental note to come back to this belief statement throughout our conversation. One way to positively address statements like this is to ask the teacher, "What would you do if you thought they could?"

PRESUME POSITIVE INTENTIONS

In addition to listening, an administrator needs to begin coaching conversations by presuming positive intentions. Teaching and coaching are incredible jobs! The days are long, but the rewards are great—when we have the patience to wait for them. As educators we must be staunch defenders of our amazing profession, this vocation that called to us and that keeps us coming back despite the many challenges. Too often we allow the judgments and criticisms of others, or worse, our own negative self-doubt, to tarnish the work we do. To combat that, I am embracing the idea of presuming positive intentions.

I don't know a single teacher or counselor or support staff member who gets up in the morning determined to ruin the lives of children. Nor do I know any administrator who gets up and skips into work, hoping to torture the adults or students with whom he or she works. But I've heard many versions of the statements above made by and about teachers and administrators.

Presuming positive intentions is the solution to those negative assumptions. It is a stance that requires us to take time to build relationships with our fellow educators so that when we don't understand their actions, we can empathize with them instead of criticize them.

As a coach, when I am working with a teacher, I want to begin every interaction presuming positive intentions. I presume that the teacher wants her students to be successful and that she wants to collaborate with me. I presume that the teacher has great ideas and, with my encouragement, can determine the best next step for student instruction. I presume that the teacher knows as much, if not more, than me. My role, therefore, as coach is to listen and ask questions that encourage the teacher to reflect on his or her own practice.

ASK THE RIGHT QUESTIONS

I begin coaching conversations with a reflective question to get the teacher talking and thinking about his or her practice. With the right questions, I can guide and elicit the teacher's best thinking. This is where my listening skills are on high alert.

Asking an open-ended, non-judgmental, reflective question can be one of the hardest skills for coaches and leaders to develop. Consider the question, *How could you create better student talk opportunities?* By including the word *better* in the question, I've made a judgment. When a teacher hears this question from a coach, he or she may immediately go into a defensive mode. We don't want coaching conversations to feel like offense versus defense.

Phrases such as "Why did you..." or "Why didn't you..." can also put someone on the defensive. Avoid judgments in your coaching questions to help teachers open up and process their work.

Now consider the question, *How can you make sure you call on the same number of boys and girls so that Juan isn't sitting silently in the back all period?*

This is another trap that coaches often fall into. Because we observed something, such as Juan sitting silently or a teacher calling on more girls than boys, we frame a question with our advice built right in. This is also not a reflective question. This can come later in a coaching conversation after a teacher has asked what you noticed during your observation.

> *"Probably my best quality as a coach is that I ask a lot of challenging questions and let the person come up with the answer."*
>
> –PHIL DIXON

Questions that begin with "Have you considered . . ." or "What if you . . ." are not reflective questions either. While these may come up later, this is not the place to begin a coaching conversation. These statements lead to you sharing ideas with the teacher before eliciting ideas from the teacher. Remember, "whoever talks the most learns the most," so consider who is doing the most learning in your coaching conversations.

Consider the following alternative, reflective examples:

- How do you ensure all students have opportunities to demonstrate their understanding of the concept?
- In what ways do you check that each student has mastery of a skill before you move on?
- How do you ensure you call on students in an equitable manner throughout your lesson?

These reflective questions presume positive intention. Instead of a teacher immediately having to defend something they did or did not do, they are asked to share a practice, routine, or structure they have developed (and we, as the coach, have presumed that they have an answer about these topics). These reflective questions are open ended. They do not lead a teacher to a specific answer, nor do they have our opinion or ideas built in.

A personal test as you practice creating reflective questions is to ask and answer them yourself. If you say yes to any of these questions, your question is not an open-ended, non-judgmental, reflective question. That doesn't mean it's a bad question; it just means you save it until a later point in a coaching conversation. Here are a few more filters to test your questions. Ask . . .

- Can a teacher answer this question saying only yes or no?
- Is there only one right answer to this question?
- Is my opinion or advice evident within this question?
- Are there judgment or opinion words within this question?
- Is my question actually a statement, not a question?
- Is there a particular answer I expect to hear?

I encourage coaches to craft a few reflective questions and write them down (on a sticky note or in a device) to carry during coaching conversations. It is hard to come up with a productive reflective question on the spot when you begin this work. Provide yourself with support by thinking of a few questions ahead of time so you are always prepared!

Here are a few more characteristics of open-ended, non-judgmental, reflective questions:

- They have multiple detailed answers based on the teacher and the circumstances.
- They lead to deeper coaching conversations based on the teacher's knowledge, strengths, and beliefs about his or her students and instructional practice.
- They build or strengthen trusting relationships between the teacher and the coach.

I recommend that a coach begins a coaching conversation with a reflective question to get the teacher talking about his or her goals.

Coaching supports a teacher's goal to improve an instructional strategy on behalf of student learning. Once the teacher has begun to share, the coach can use active listening to guide the conversation into a productive dialogue that leads to action. One of the most critical skills a coach can learn and practice is the art of questioning. And it truly is an art when it comes to a teacher-coach relationship.

One of the most critical skills a coach can learn and practice is the art of questioning.

Once the coaching conversation is underway, there are all sorts of questions a coach can ask. Questioning is a critical tool for an instructional coach because once the coach poses the question, the teacher is doing the thinking work by answering. The coach's role continues to be that of the active listener, determining where to steer the conversation next based on what the teacher says (or doesn't say).

Here are some additional types of questions to ask as you coach. This list is meant as a starting point and not an exhaustive supply.

- **Factual questions**—Ask details about standards, lesson planning, students, etc.:
    - » On what standard will you focus for this lesson?
    - » How many of your students need a scaffold to be successful during this lesson?

- **Yes and No questions**—Simple questions that allow a teacher to feel comfortable about the topic at hand by first starting with easy questions to answer:
    - » Have you read this text before?
    - » Do you know the Lexile level of this text?
    - » Do you have the manipulatives you need for this math lesson?

- **Clarifying questions**—Important follow-up questions to ensure the teacher and the coach have a common understanding of the elements of instruction and learning:
    - » Can you tell me more about the struggles you observed your students having during the lesson?

» What student behaviors bothered you?

» What do you mean by engagement during a lesson?

- **Reflective questions**—Open-ended questions created to help the teacher reflect on his or her practice:
    » How do you feel about the lesson?

    » Why do you think the students were successful?

    » What will you do tomorrow based on what your students produced today?

- **Wondering statements**—Not technically a question but a statement that is shared in hopes that a teacher can reflect on a particular topic:
    » I wonder what might happen if we had the students talk to their partners before we ask them to write.

    » What do you think might happen if we don't provide that scaffold?

- **Loaded invitations**—I'm borrowing this concept from Katie Wood Ray's book *Study Driven: A Framework for Planning Units of Study in the Writing Workshop*. A loaded invitation presupposes that someone is thinking about a particular topic:
    » What are you thinking about student engagement during your read alouds?

    » What are you thinking about providing more independence for students?

A coach must be skilled enough to know which type of question will work in any particular coaching conversation and be able to think on the fly. I always encourage coaches to write down some sample questions or question stems for themselves before going into any coaching conversation, especially if they know themselves well enough to know that this isn't yet an area of strength for them. More importantly, it is best for a coach to take time to prepare for a coaching conversation. Whether the conversation comes after an observation, or it's based on a teacher request for support, the coach should go into the meeting armed with a variety of questions as well as resources that might be useful.

The best way to improve your questioning skills is to practice. This involves a lot of listening! While role-playing makes many people (especially *introverts*!) uncomfortable, this can be an important tool to support coaches in their questioning skills. I encourage you to find a trusted colleague with whom you can practice active listening and open-ended, non-judgmental, reflective questions.

I had a recent exchange with a teacher that once again highlighted the importance of listening. Mari, the teacher, and I were meeting during her prep to co-write a blog about a recent district experience. She invited me to come early to our meeting, so I could observe part of her science lesson that day. I was able to see a fun lab about plate tectonics, where I spoke to most of the student groups and saw their final products for the day. When the class was over, the teacher asked me what I thought. I, being a coach at all times, turned the question back to her and asked her how she felt the lesson had gone.

The teacher spoke for a while, and in her answer, I heard a concern about how long it took students to clean up the lab. Based on that information, I shared something positive that I noticed the teacher had done during that chaotic clean-up time. I then said something like, "I hear some frustration about the length of the clean-up time and the behavior of some students during that time. What do you think might make the process more organized?" The teacher realized she had group roles (on beautifully laminated lanyards) that they had used in the past, but she hadn't considered using them for this lab. I asked if using those roles would assist in the clean-up process, and she thought they would. The next day we had the Twitter exchange shown on the next page.

There is so much that I appreciate about this simple exchange that we had over Twitter. First, I am not on Mari's campus regularly, so my observation was short and not designed to be a formal observation or an official coaching session. Because we have a trusting relationship, however, she invited me into her room to observe. It was also where she welcomed specific feedback from me. Second, Mari felt comfortable enough to share her success with me (and the Twitterverse) the next day. And finally, I love that she reflected on what coaching is supposed to be in a simple concise way: observation, feedback, implementation, and reflection. This

Mari Venturino
@MsVenturino

I'm thankful @AmyLIllingworth came a little early for our meeting yesterday and had a chance to observe my class. I got some valuable feedback, and implemented it today! #suhsd #vikingslearn #observeme

10:04am · 19 Apr 2018 · Twitter Web Client

1 REPLY 1 RETWEET 6 LIKES

Reply to @MsVenturino @AmyLIlling...

Amy Illingworth, EdD @AmyLIl... 21h
Replying to @MsVenturino
What did you implement today?! How did it go?

Mari Venturino @MsVenturino 16h
Replying to @AmyLIllingworth
Lab group roles. Clean up went so well!

Amy Illingworth, EdD @AmyLIl... 15h
Replying to @MsVenturino
Awesome!! I'm proud of you for taking action right away.

Mari Venturino @MsVenturino 15h
Replying to @AmyLIllingworth
Isn't that how coaching is supposed to happen? (Real, not rhetorical, question.) Observation, feedback, implementation, reflection.

Amy Illingworth, EdD @AmyLIl... 15h
Replying to @MsVenturino
Can I quote this in my book?!?!

Mari Venturino @MsVenturino 14h
Replying to @AmyLIllingworth
Most definitely! 😄

happened because I listened to her reflection about a struggle she saw. If I had begun our conversation telling her what she did right and wrong and what I thought she should change, this would have ended very differently. But I began our conversation with an open-ended reflective question, and then I listened. The teacher did the rest of the work!

CHOOSE THE COACH ADVENTURE

If you have just arrived from Chapter Eleven and are curious about how Mr. Fox takes his organized calendar and uses it to provide teachers feedback, keep reading.

If you have just arrived from Chapter Eight where Ms. Martinez was in the middle of a Lesson Study, skip down to continue her story.

PRINCIPAL FOX

Mr. Fox had just put a time-management plan into place, complete with an organized calendar and clear expectations for his secretaries. As he began to visit classrooms, he wanted to provide feedback to teachers. After reflecting his first few conversations, he realized that he had done most of the talking. Before meeting with another teacher, Mr. Fox drafted a few sample reflective questions to ask his teachers and get them to do more of the talking. He began his next debrief with a teacher by saying, "I enjoyed visiting your room earlier today during your science lesson. What do you think went well for your students today?" The question prompted the teacher to reflect and share things Mr. Fox may have missed before or after he visited. After a while, Mr. Fox said, "I know your grade level has been focusing on students' academic language use. How do you provide opportunities for students to use science vocabulary in their oral or written language?" The conversation continued, with Mr. Fox spending less and less time talking as he listened to the teacher's reflection. By the end of their chat, the teacher has realized that with a little more structure, her partner talk opportunities could require students to use academic language in more meaningful ways.

- To learn more about how Mr. Fox uses his listening skills to build teacher leadership capacity, go to Chapter Four: What Is the Role of a Teacher Leader as an Instructional Coach?
- To learn more about how Mr. Fox revisits his purpose for wanting to coach his teachers, go to Chapter One: Why Do We Need Instructional Leadership Coaching?

PRINCIPAL MARTINEZ

At Learning for All High School, we last left Principal Martinez right in the heat of a challenging moment with a math team. They were in the middle of a lesson study debrief when a teacher, Ms. Smith, challenged the process by asking, "This is ridiculous. Is no one going to address the fact that you changed the lesson we had planned together? What was the point of planning if you were just going to do whatever you wanted to do anyway?" Ms. Martinez took a moment to reflect, realizing how important her listening and coaching skills were going to be for her right now.

She said, "Thank you for bringing this up. Let's talk about the in-the-moment decision we made during the lesson to make a change." She went on to ask her co-teacher questions, so they could explain what they had been thinking and why they chose to implement the engagement strategy that wasn't part of the lesson plan. She then asked the group, "When we used that engagement strategy, what did you observe students saying or doing?" While Ms. Smith was quiet for a while, the other teachers all shared observational notes about students talking, students using math language, students explaining their reasoning to others, and about how many students were engaged during that time.

Ms. Martinez let the group talk for a few minutes while she quietly observed the teacher who had brought up the concern. She wanted to bring the teacher back into the conversation, so she said, "Ms. Smith, what did you observe students doing?" Ms. Smith was able to share an exchange she heard between two students. Ms. Martinez thanked her for sharing and said, "What might have happened if we hadn't added that engagement strategy into our lesson?" The group was able to discuss this, noting that they would not have heard many students using math language appropriately nor students explaining their thinking. The group, including Ms. Smith, was able to recognize the value of the on-the-spot decision the teachers had made and how it had benefited students.

By listening and asking a variety of questions, Ms. Martinez was able to help the team reflect on the process as they considered a valid concern from one of the teachers. After the lesson study, Ms. Martinez approached Ms. Smith privately. She wanted to check in with the teacher, knowing that the lesson study process had been outside of her comfort zone. Through their conversation, Ms. Smith shared that it had been an uncomfortable morning for her but that she appreciated the conversation because it helped her realize the value of listening to student talk as a way to check for understanding. Ms. Smith also shared that she was used to planning a lesson and following it through to the end and had a hard time deviating from her plans. This honest reflection gave Ms. Martinez insight into Ms. Smith's planning process and an area of growth on which to work with her—in the moment formative assessment.

After this conversation, Ms. Martinez went back to the assistant principal who had observed her facilitate the lesson study. She asked the assistant principal what he thought about the process. He told her he thought it was a lot of work for not much benefit.

This shocked Ms. Martinez. She used her questioning techniques to prompt him for more information, but he really didn't have much more to say. When she asked him very specific questions, such as "What did you notice about Ms. Smith at the beginning of the process versus at the end?" The assistant principal couldn't respond. He hadn't noticed the change in her attitude, and he hadn't heard some of her later comments.

Ms. Martinez spent some time reflecting on the conversation with her assistant principal. She knew she could call her coach for support, but she wished she could speak to another high school principal about what she was facing. How would another principal work with an assistant principal like this?

- To find out what Ms. Martinez does next, go to Chapter Nine: Who Is in Your PLN?

Chapter Eight
HOW CAN LESSON STUDY SUPPORT COACHING?

You develop shared depth through continuous learning, by solving problems, and by getting better and better at what you do.
—MICHAEL FULLAN

After spending ten years at the middle and high school levels as a teacher, peer coach, and assistant principal, I became an elementary school principal. I was a passionate instructional leader who knew that one of my most important roles was to be in classrooms supporting my teachers as they helped our students learn and grow. To demonstrate my knowledge to teachers who didn't think I could support them (because I had never taught primary grades), I had to roll up my sleeves and do the work alongside them. I did this in a number of ways: visiting all classrooms and providing written and verbal feedback to teachers, participating in PLC discussions, and creating a structure for grade levels to participate in lesson studies.

Lesson studies became a way to build a learning community as a staff and to demonstrate that I was an instructional leader and a coach. My involvement showed that I was there to support my teachers as they supported our students. This structure also provided me a way in which to develop shared instructional leadership across teams of teachers in meaningful ways. What follows explains how we structured lesson studies, a process that was created in Japan as an instructional tool for collaborative learning.

SET THE GOAL AND THE EXPECTATION

A team of teachers would have a substitute take over their classes for a full day in order to complete a lesson study. In the beginning, I would facilitate the work, though it was my goal for the site literacy coach or teacher leaders to take on that role once they had experienced the process. We would begin the day setting the expectation. There was always one instructional or curricular area in which a grade level wanted more focused support—small group instruction, engagement during read alouds, structured partner talk using academic language, etc.—that would be established before the meeting. The facilitator would review the focus area and the current data of the class in which the lesson would be taught. Reviewing the data is a critical step in helping teachers cross the bridge between formative assessment and instruction—a bridge that is made of data analysis and purposeful planning. Once the group had a sense of the students' needs and the focus area, we would begin to plan a lesson.

The first thing I made clear to the team was that we were collaboratively planning a lesson for this particular class, and we wouldn't decide who would teach the lesson (though it could be one or more of us co-teaching) until after it was fully planned. In my school, we were using a common planning document to support lesson planning, so we all had a copy of that document as well as the curricular resources for the grade level and content.

DEFINE THE FOCUS AND A COMMON LANGUAGE

Our process became a truly collaborative discussion as we went through each area of what we had defined as a staff as crucial elements to a strong lesson. The discussions became richer when teams were comfortable enough for members to disagree with one another. When teachers have to justify their thinking, whether it is about where to chunk a text for a shared reading or what type of sentence frame to create to support partner talk, they begin to see what elements of their repertoire have purpose and meaning for students and which elements are things they have always done "just because." It is so powerful for teachers to have to find their own voice and a common language to explain the work they do in isolation in their classrooms. If a school has a specific professional development focus, this is a great way for the group to discuss that focus and what it looks like in a lesson plan.

Until we had these types of conversations, when someone said, "student engagement," each staff member was operating under their own understanding of that phrase. Through lesson studies, we were able to collaboratively craft definitions that framed our instructional program.

The facilitator often has a tough job during the planning of the lesson. You must keep the group focused on the task, aware of the time, and ensure that all participants have a voice. At some point, you must make sure everyone has a complete lesson recorded, so any one of them would feel comfortable teaching the lesson as planned. Once the plan has been created, the facilitator helps the group determine who will be the actual teacher (or co-teachers) of the lesson. Part of this discussion centers around the purpose: We developed a lesson as a team; we want to see it in action, observe the students, and then determine what works well for students and what needs revising. With new teams or a school that is new to this process, I recommend that the principal or coach volunteer to teach the first round. Teaching the lesson gave me "street cred" with a staff who didn't yet know me well and took the pressure off the teachers, who had never experienced any sort of peer observations. Whenever possible, I encouraged the team to co-teach, with various members taking on parts of the lesson to share the load and have more ownership of the teaching.

TEACH OR OBSERVE THE LESSON

Next, the entire group would go into the selected class to teach the lesson. Anyone not delivering instruction was responsible for sitting as close to students as possible to record what they were saying or doing throughout the lesson. We set clear expectations for the observers during this time, even ensuring that we were spread out around the room to record as much anecdotal notes about students as possible.

DEBRIEF

After teaching the lesson, the entire group returns to the planning room to debrief. The facilitator ensures that the conversation is about the implementation of the group lesson plan and not an evaluation of the teacher(s) who delivered the lesson. Student work and quotes are critical evidence to help teachers analyze the effectiveness of the actual lesson as it relates to student performance. The facilitator must also make sure to bring the conversation back to the instructional focus of the school, so teachers can discuss what that focus looks like in action in the classroom.

The second part of the debrief involves the application phase. The team members discuss what this particular class needs next, following up on this lesson. They also discuss how they would adapt this particular lesson to meet the needs of their specific students (in classes that haven't yet received this lesson). This can lead to one of two things: The teachers make a commitment to try the lesson in their own room the next day, or the entire team revises the lesson and goes directly into another room to teach it again (I would not recommend this for your first round of lesson study but for future stages when the planning phase can be done with a more experienced team). The team would then follow up on their own lessons at their next PLC meeting.

The final—and truly significant—stage of lesson study is to debrief the process of the work. Teachers, as adult learners, need time to reflect on the collaborative nature of planning, observing, and debriefing a lesson as a group. The goal is that the teachers find value in the process to improve their own instructional performance, their collaboration with their team, and ultimately their students' performance. When the team becomes hungry for more collaboration time, asks for more time to conduct lesson studies on their own, and begins to explore peer observations, you know they value the process.

I believe the lesson study process is a powerful tool in the box of an instructional leader and coach. My teachers enjoyed it so much that I requested we conduct a lesson study on a day we were scheduled for a formal compliance observation (during a time in California when Reading First schools had check-up visits to ensure we were using the adopted curriculum with fidelity). Normally these visits involved me, as the site principal, leading a team of observers and district leaders into all primary classrooms for quick visits; instead, our first-grade team volunteered to conduct a lesson study live in front of our visitors, from planning to co-teaching to debriefing. Our visitors were impressed with the process and with the open dialogue about instruction and student learning that took place throughout the lesson study. I was so proud of our team on that day and happy that their work was celebrated publicly.

CHOOSE THE COACH ADVENTURE

If you have just arrived from Chapter Four, keep reading to learn about Mr. Fox's next steps for building teacher leadership capacity.

If you have just arrived from Chapter Four where Ms. Martinez's team was building teacher leadership through focused coaching, skip down to continue your journey with Principal Martinez.

PRINCIPAL FOX

We left Mr. Fox with the beginning of a demonstration classroom available for coaching and with some staff members trying out the #ObserveMe challenge. He decides to try a lesson study with one of his grade-level teams. He approaches the demonstration classroom teacher first, explaining to her what a lesson study is. She likes the idea and thinks her team would be interested in participating. She volunteers her own classroom for the study. Together Mr. Fox and the teacher share the idea with the rest of the team. Everyone agrees to try this new learning, and they pick a day they can arrange for substitutes to cover their class.

Principal Fox feels nervous on the day of the lesson study. He's stepping out of his comfort zone to try a new coaching strategy that is testing his own knowledge. He arrives early that day and spends some time reflecting in his office before the day begins.

Reminding himself that whatever happens will be a learning experience for everyone helps settle his nerves. He also remembers that he doesn't have to be perfect; he just needs to try and listen and support.

While Mr. Fox officially facilitates the lesson study, the demonstration classroom teacher truly takes the lead throughout the day. She has extensive pedagogical knowledge, and her peers appreciate the way she shares ideas and suggestions. She never takes over the conversation and is skilled at bringing others into the dialogue. The team really wants her to teach the collaboratively designed lesson, but Mr. Fox encourages the group to co-teach. Each team member agrees to take on a portion of the lesson.

The lesson they had co-planned is a success, and the team comes back to the planning room excited to discuss what went well. Mr. Fox has to remind himself to avoid judgment language and to focus on the debrief on the evidence of what students learned. When it is all said and done, Principal Fox realizes his teachers are ready for so much more. They are open to trying new ideas and collaborating. Now he needs to focus his energy on his coaching plan.

- To learn more about Mr. Fox's coaching model, go to Chapter Five: What Is a Coaching Theory of Action?

PRINCIPAL MARTINEZ

When we left LAHS, Ms. Martinez and her team were busy building teacher leadership capacity through coaching. On her own, Ms. Martinez had done some professional reading about a process called lesson study. She decided that this professional development process would be a great next step for the math department. Ms. Martinez introduced the idea to the teacher leader with whom she was working who agreed it could be great and volunteered her own classroom. In the next PLC meeting, Ms. Martinez and the teacher brought up the idea to the entire team, and they were all willing to use their PLC release day for this process in the morning as long as they had team planning time in the afternoon.

Ms. Martinez had one of the assistant principals observe her as she facilitated the process with this math PLC. She wanted to build the capacity of her administrative team but realized that it could be overwhelming if four administrators were present all day.

The lesson study was not perfect, as this was a team who didn't always agree on curricular resources or instructional strategies. Ms. Martinez worked hard as the facilitator to guide the group to a common lesson plan but was challenged through each step of the process. When they went into the room to teach the lesson, she and the teacher who had volunteered attempted to co-teach the lesson. While teaching, they did some on-the-spot adjustments to the lesson, bringing in an engagement strategy that the PLC hadn't agreed to use during their planning session. Ms. Martinez was hoping that the other teachers would see the value of this strategy based on how much student talk it produced.

During the lesson debrief, the teacher who had co-taught shared her reflections and some aha! moments she'd had with her students based on what they did and did not do during the lesson. Two other teachers were able to share observational notes that added to the discussion. The fourth teacher was silent for a long time until she finally said, "This is ridiculous. Is no one going to address the fact that you changed the lesson we had planned together? What was the point of planning if you were just going to do whatever you wanted to do anyway?" Ms. Martinez was in a tough spot. How should she proceed?

- To find out what Ms. Martinez does next, go to Chapter Seven: Who Is Listening the Most?

Part III

Creating a Coaching Community

None of us can do this work alone. Improving student achievement through instructional coaching is hard, but it's important work for our students and teachers. Creating a community of practice for instructional leaders provides much-needed support. I invite you to join our community with #CoachADV on Twitter to find others reading and discussing the important work of instructional coaching. As you explore this section of the book, consider who is already in your community and what kind of additions you would like to make, so your community will be even stronger and more supportive.

Part III

Creating an Inspiring Community

CHAPTER NINE
WHO IS IN YOUR PLN?

Collaboration allows us to know more than we are
capable of knowing by ourselves.

–PAUL SOLARZ

Human beings crave interaction. We are social creatures who learn from communication with others. But being an administrator can be isolating! If you are an elementary principal, you might be the only administrator on your campus. Ditto if you are an instructional coach at a site. Many middle and high school principals are lucky to have a small team of fellow administrators around them. District leaders are often the only director of curriculum or director of technology as well. So how do we, as leaders who want to be instructional coaches, surround ourselves with support? How do we create a community of practice for our own learning and growth?

JOIN THE TWITTERVERSE
One way I encourage all leaders to grow their community is to build a professional learning network, or a PLN. This is often accomplished via online connections through social media. During the past five years, I have grown my PLN on Twitter by learning how to use hashtags, participating in Twitter chats, reading and responding to blogs written by educators, creating my own blog and sharing it publicly, and connecting with other educators from around

the world. At the same time, I have expanded my local network by using Twitter to tell our district's story—using a district hashtag to share successes from various schools—and creating a monthly district Twitter chat. By using the hashtag #CoachADV, my goal is to continue to expand my coaching community online by sharing instructional coaching ideas and learning from others who are on their own coaching adventure.

Using a common hashtag allows us to collectively build our understanding, share our challenges, and help each other grow. Once you begin to interact in a hashtag, you find other educators to follow. This is a way to build a community of practice around yourself because these educators are often in similar roles as you and face similar struggles. If you have not yet made the leap to join Twitter, I encourage you to pause in your reading and create a Twitter account right now. Consider this part of your coaching adventure!

FIND (OR CREATE) ONLINE AND IN-PERSON COMMUNITIES

Another way to build a community of practice is to reach out, virtually or in person, to other instructional coaches in positions like yours. As an administrator, each school in your district, county, or region has at least one administrator with whom you can connect. If you are embarking on the instructional coaching role on your own, it's important you connect with others somewhere who are doing this work. Join a listserv or virtual group, read professional journals, and find ways to surround yourself with other instructional coaches. Being able to call, text, Vox, or email a colleague when you are struggling or when you have a breakthrough is important. The work of coaching can be isolating if you are the only coach in your school, district, or area. By building a community, you will have support when times are challenging, friends with whom to share your successes, and a place to go with questions and to share great ideas.

As a new principal, I moved to a new district. My district didn't offer a lot of support for new administrators, but I was lucky in that two other new principals were hired that same year. We quickly formed a support group; in addition, one of the veteran principals in the district reached out to us and scheduled regular meetings during which she would share some amazing resources with us. Once I had my feet under me in the new job, I realized there weren't a lot of opportunities for me to expand my leadership knowledge, so I started a book study and invited all my fellow principals. We kept the structure loose enough that it didn't feel like another demand on our already busy schedules but tight enough that we helped hold each other accountable for learning and trying out new ideas at our schools. This was one way to build my professional learning network and feel supported in an isolated job.

ESTABLISH AN ON-SITE TEAM

Creating a team of teacher leaders at your site is also an empowering way to build a community of practice whose collective role is to improve student learning at your site. This might be called an instructional leadership team (ILT) or school leadership team (SLT) or another acronym that makes sense in your context (For the sake of continuity, I will refer to this as an ILT.). Some teachers' bargaining units, or unions, have something like this written into their contract. In other places, principals or district leaders decide to create this team for monthly meetings centered around fulfilling the school vision and helping each student within the system succeed. An ILT is often comprised of a teacher from each grade level, content area, and specialty programs as well as the principal. An ILT can also include a counselor and a representative from your support staff.

Once you've established your ILT, you can facilitate instructional conversations about your student achievement data, your instructional goals as a site, and the systems you have or need to put into place to support teachers and staff supporting students. This is also a way to introduce your role as an instructional coach to the teachers. The teachers on your ILT may be the first you can approach through the instructional coach lens. They are also most likely to be the first teachers willing to participate in peer observations or a lesson study.

If you are a district-level leader, it is important that you have developed a system for support. If your district has a coaching position with a job description, where there is a coach at every site, this team of coaches will need support. In order to ensure you have consistency in the role and coherence across your district, create a system that supports coaches. When I was a director of educational services, I oversaw the instructional coaches we had in each of our schools. Each coach was co-evaluated by their site principal and by me. In order to create a PLN for our instructional coaches, I put a number of structures in place to support them.

MONTHLY MEETINGS

First, we had monthly meetings. During these face-to-face workshops, we read research, including a year-long book study of Elena Aguilar's *The Art of Coaching*. We also discussed coaching successes and challenges. We practiced coaching, using role-playing to hone our active listening and reflective questioning skills. I also encouraged them to create and expand their own PLN by having them each sign up for Twitter. We did this together in our meeting so that those who needed extra help got the hands-on support right then. Once everyone had an account, we held a Twitter chat while we were together in the same room. I had Twitter veterans at each table to support their colleagues throughout our chat. This was an easy, non-threatening way to introduce the coaches to ways they could use Twitter and interact with others during a chat.

REGULAR COMMUNICATION

In between those monthly meetings, I relied on a number of supports to build and maintain community. I sent out a weekly email with important dates, information, and updates from around the district, links to coaching articles, and questions for coaches to ponder. We held monthly Twitter chats about coaching, so we could connect virtually in between our workshops. Over time, different coaches from the team facilitated those chats.

IN-PERSON COLLABORATION AND PRACTICE

I scheduled regular visits to each of the schools to meet with the coaches at those sites. While there, the coaches and I would visit classrooms together. After each observation, we stepped outside and discussed what instructional practices we observed that were positively impacting student learning. Then we would practice reflective questions we could ask the teachers.

I have also modeled a coaching conversation where the coach is able to observe me coaching a teacher we previously observed. I do this with new coaches and new assistant principals to support their understanding of our district's coaching model.

MORE TIPS FOR SUPPORTING INSTRUCTIONAL COACHES

What is important when supporting instructional coaches? What does professional development for coaches look like? Here are my top tips for supporting the learning of coaches:

- **Build in time for reflection.** Reflection is a critical element for any professional and one that is often pushed aside due to time constraints. By providing reflection time for coaches that includes independent writing, collaborative discussion, and goal setting, you are well on your way to ensuring coaches make a true impact in their work. I begin and end each of our coach sessions with reflection time.
- **Make sure everyone has a voice and choice.** I strongly believe that all learners, whether students, teachers, coaches, or administrators, deserve to have a voice and a choice about their professional growth. In coaching sessions, this can take the form of coaches choosing their own groups and topics when designing professional development modules.
- **Model lifelong learning.** In education, we love to say we are lifelong learners. I take this to heart and model that belief when designing the sessions with our coaches. Here are just a few of the things we've learned through authentic practice during our sessions:
  - » How to use Twitter to hold a Twitter chat about coaching
  - » How to find and save educational blogs in an RSS feed or Feedly
  - » How to write a blog for our district learning blog
  - » How to design a CCSS-aligned model lesson using a rich piece of literature

- » How to use Google Docs for collaboration and communication
- » How to use various protocols for discussing professional texts
- » Plus so much more!

- **Learning takes time.** Coaches are often expected to support anywhere from three to eight grade levels and multiple content areas. They are also expected to be leaders with strong content and pedagogical knowledge. Learning all of that to a deep enough knowledge to be able to coach and support colleagues in each area takes time. At each of our coach sessions, I build in time for discussing the professional reading we do. Not only did we continue to model learning by using a protocol for guiding the discussion, but we also provided enough time for the coaches to truly have an in-depth discussion. We were practicing what the Common Core Speaking and Listening Standard 1 asks of our students. To have a collaborative conversation, you need to read and prepare ahead of time and then be ready to build on others' ideas as part of a rich collaboration.

- **Celebrate successes.** It is so important to honor the hard work that coaches do each day to support the instructional practices of teachers across their school or district. I love to include celebrations as part of our coaching sessions. Celebrating publicly helps to spread the word of the good work we are accomplishing toward our district goals and to recognize that success looks different for each of us. Highlight successes, no matter how big or small—especially during times of significant change, such as the full implementation of the Common Core State Standards across your district. Doing so keeps people feeling positive during challenging times.

I am passionate about professional development and coaching for all educators. These tips can help facilitate ongoing, job-embedded professional development for instructional coaches within any educational system.

If your district has a coach position at all schools, join forces as a community together regardless of whether the district brings you together regularly. You can meet up for coffee and coaching chats, or you can create a Google Classroom for virtual connections and sharing of resources. When you are the lone coach on your campus, whether as an administrator or a teacher leader, it is important that you find ways to get yourself support throughout your learning. No one is an expert in this; we all benefit from coaching and support. Go out and build your PLN today! Find your community with us at #CoachADV!

CHOOSE THE COACH ADVENTURE

If you have just arrived from the Introduction and are curious about those to whom Mr. Fox reaches out for help as he dives into planning a PD day with his staff, or if you've come from Chapter Two, where Mr. Fox was learning his coaching skills to get into rooms, continue his story here.

If you've just arrived from Chapter Seven where Ms. Martinez was struggling with one of her assistant principals, skip down to read more of the story.

PRINCIPAL FOX

Mr. Fox was just told by his boss that he does not have a budget to hire an outside consultant for the upcoming professional development day. He knows he is going to have to plan something for his staff, but he doesn't know where or how to start. He has also begun to visit classrooms, but his primary teachers feel like he is picking on them and ignoring his upper grades. He is scared to visit more rooms until he creates a new plan.

Mr. Fox recently read a professional book with a few of his principal colleagues. He pulls that book off the shelf, flips through it, and decides to call one of the other elementary principals in his district. They have a discussion, first about the book, and then about the upcoming PD day. Mr. Fox's colleague explains that he had met with his teacher leadership team to plan the day based on their site goals. The other principal mentions that he based his team's planning agenda on something he saw on Twitter. Mr. Fox takes copious notes as his colleague speaks, but when he hangs up the phone, he is still unsure of what to do next.

He decides to log onto Twitter for a moment. He's been using Twitter for a while to follow some news outlets to stay current on world and local events, but he hasn't used it for educational purposes. When his colleague mentioned Twitter, Mr. Fox decided to give it a try. He began by following the authors of some of the professional books he has in his office. He then begins to read some of their tweets, which leads him to read a whole lot of blogs written by these same authors and others. Soon Mr. Fox has an idea for how to bring together a group of teacher leaders to discuss the upcoming PD day. He thinks he can also talk to them about his classroom visits. He doesn't want to lose track of these new blogs, so Mr. Fox sets up a Feedly account that he can log into at any time to read the recently published blog posts of his favorite blog writers. He also sets a goal for himself to check Twitter at least once a day for his own learning.

- To learn about how Mr. Fox handles his teacher leadership meeting and PD planning, go to Chapter One: Why Do We Need Instructional Leadership Coaching?
- To learn about how Mr. Fox plans his professional development, go to Chapter Ten: How Do Coaches Facilitate Collaborative Professional Learning?

PRINCIPAL MARTINEZ

Principal Martinez is struggling with how to coach one of her assistant principals. She is looking to brainstorm ideas with someone in a similar position to her. She decides to participate in a Twitter chat (#LeadLAP) with other leaders as motivation and support for herself. At the end of the hour-long chat, she realizes there is one person with whom she has really connected whose answers are still resonating with her. Ms. Martinez decides to send a personal message to this person, Ms. X, through Twitter.

Ms. Martinez received a response and began to communicate with Ms. X, who was also a high school principal. After several messages through Twitter and email, the two began to converse on the phone. These conversations were a great support for Ms. Martinez; It was helpful to have someone who understood the context of her work. Ms. X was struggling with a challenging budget situation and was seeking advice from Ms. Martinez. When Ms. Martinez shared her struggles with her assistant principal, her new friend was able to provide a number of suggestions for her to try.

While this was going on, Ms. Martinez was also using Twitter to support her staff who were holding a weekly chat and sharing best practices through their school hashtag. When she began to retweet and share the good work being done by her staff, she began to hear from more people in her PLN outside of her school. Other leaders reached out to ask her how she had gotten so many teachers on Twitter to share their work. One leader shared how he was using #ObserveMe as an assistant principal. Ms. Martinez took this idea back to her leadership team, and her assistant principals loved the idea! Ms. Martinez also found some new professional resources to read and share with her staff—all from her Twitter PLN.

One of the biggest benefits to this interactive PLN was accountability. After a few weeks without contact, Ms. X reached out to Ms. Martinez to share a budget success and to check in with the assistant principal situation. Ms. Martinez was sad to report that she hadn't made much progress with her assistant principal. Ms. X was a great sounding board, but she also held Ms. Martinez's feet to the fire. She said, "Look, I know how hard this is. But this guy is not as effective as he could be, and it's up to you to be honest with him. Have you picked one growth area on which you want him to focus? Communicate that to him tomorrow and set up a plan for next steps. I will call you tomorrow night to check back in."

Ms. Martinez appreciated the push from her friend, and she met with her assistant principal the next day. They created an action plan with three items he had to complete in the next two weeks. They scheduled a follow-up meeting, so he could report back on his progress. Ms. Martinez was happy when she was able to share this with Ms. X, who did call the next day. Ms. Martinez thanked her friend for stepping off the Twitter screen and reaching out personally. It made all the difference.

- To reflect on Ms. Martinez's journey and your own coaching adventure, go to Chapter Thirteen: What Is Your Coaching Adventure?
- If you haven't begun to follow Mr. Fox's journey yet, go to the Introduction to begin a new adventure.

Chapter Ten

HOW DO COACHES FACILITATE COLLABORATIVE PROFESSIONAL LEARNING?

When educators fail to pay careful attention to teacher learning in schools, conditions of teaching and learning remain the same. Only through learning will individuals change and grow.

–STEPHANIE HIRSH AND TRACY CROW,
Becoming a Learning Team: A Guide to a Teacher-Led
Cycle of Continuous Improvement

One of the roles of an instructional coach is to facilitate professional learning for those we coach. In my first few years as a teacher, most of the professional learning I experienced was a lot of me sitting and listening to someone telling me what to do in my classroom. After a few years of that, I got lucky when I moved onto a new school where I experienced a very different kind of professional learning.

My first experience working with an instructional coach was positive and powerful because it was based on my personal needs. I was teaching middle school English (among other things), and I worked closely with a teacher who is now one of my best friends. My partner teacher and I were able to work with a coach, Laura, who met with us to determine what our professional goals were. Since we planned together every week, it was easy to bring her into our planning sessions to help. But her help was different from what I was expecting.

When Laura joined us, she asked questions. And not just one or two questions. She asked us tons of questions. Questions like why we were using a particular text, how had we decided on a unit of study, what did we know about our students as writers, etc. At first I was taken aback by all the questions, and I felt the need to get defensive about our choices. Now I know that what Laura was doing was facilitating our learning through her questions. The more questions she asked, the more we had to talk. The more we talked, the more we made revisions to our planning, going deeper with what we expected of our students and gaining clarity around our purpose. We had the answers; she just helped us piece them together.

Based on my experience with Laura, here are a few reflective questions for you to consider when you facilitate professional learning:

- What questions could you ask to determine the professional goals of the teachers with whom you work?
- How often do you, as a coach, ask questions?
- How much wait time do you provide to ensure that you do not answer your own questions?
- What types of questions do you find most powerful for reflection?
- How do you stop yourself from taking over a conversation by talking too much?
- How can the skill of questioning enhance your coaching?

If your coaching adventure has not already taken you to the chapter about listening and questioning (Chapter Seven), you might want to jump back and read or revisit that chapter for more details on the importance of questioning and the different types of questions a coach can ask.

One of the most important things you can do as an instructional coach is realize that your role is to facilitate professional learning for those you coach. There are a number of ways you can facilitate that learning: professional learning communities (PLCs), learning walks, instructional rounds, workshops, lesson studies, and individual coaching, which we discussed in the last section.

Professional learning communities (PLCs) have looked differently everywhere I've worked. The ideal format and purpose of a PLC is that teachers have a common prep or planning period daily or weekly in which they meet to discuss instructional strategies, student progress, and lesson planning to meet students' needs. The PLC model, which was originally created by Richard and Rebecca DuFour, includes the four key areas of focus:

- What do we expect our students to know and be able to do?
- How will we know they are learning?
- How will we respond when they don't learn?
- How will we respond if they already know it?

PLC

An instructional coach can be a participating member of a PLC, especially if he or she is a part-time teacher as well. A coach can also be a facilitator of a PLC. When a coach takes on the role of facilitation in a PLC, it's important to remember that this does not mean they are the leader or the lone expert in the room. The role of a facilitator is to keep the group focused on the agenda, maintain the norms established by the group, ask reflective questions to prompt deeper discussion, and help the group work through conflict.

I often see coaches make mistakes when they step into this role. Sometimes the mistakes begin when a principal demands that a coach "fix that PLC." If a coach is asked to step in or take over a PLC on behalf of an administrator, the coach is often set up to fail. This is equally true if an administrator enters a PLC determined to "fix it." By design, PLCs are a professional learning community by teachers for teachers. This means that a coach needs to tread lightly by beginning as a participant or a facilitator as he or she learns the dynamics of a particular team.

If your school does have a dysfunctional team in need of assistance, there are ways a coach can support the team without taking it over. A coach can serve as a process observer for a PLC. When a team is not following their own norms, it's hard for one of the members to point this out to his or her colleagues. When a neutral observer, the coach, comes in and says he or she will observe the process of the team, take notes on how the members communicate, and give the team feedback at the end of the meeting, the team might be more open to hearing the feedback. The coach should then capture in writing the questions or statements that are asked and shared throughout the meeting, who participates and how often, if and when the norms are broken by group members, and anything else of relevance to helping the team function more cohesively. When the coach shares the observations at the end of the meeting, he or she should be careful not to call out individually or negatively, but rather share facts and general statements especially related to the norms of the group. If someone doesn't participate in the meeting, an appropriate way to mention this might be, "One of your norms is for all participants to have an equal voice. I observed that one member didn't speak much after the first few minutes of the meeting. How do you ensure that all participants have an equal voice throughout each meeting?"

Another way a coach can have a role in PLCs at a school is by modeling during staff meetings and professional development workshops. The coach can bring a group of teachers together to model a functioning PLC in a fishbowl type of situation. In this scenario, the small group would role-play a short PLC meeting in front of the larger staff. The coach could then facilitate discussion amongst the rest of the staff about what they observed and what their own PLCs need in the way of support.

LEARNING WALKS AND INSTRUCTIONAL ROUNDS

Many schools have begun to create their own versions of learning walks or instructional rounds. The concept of instructional rounds originally came from the book *Instructional Rounds in Education* by Elizabeth A. City, Richard Elmore, Sarah E. Fiarman, and Lee Teitel, who took the idea of medical rounds and brought it to education. No matter the name, the purpose of these walks is for a group of educators to get together, visit classrooms to observe teaching and learning in action, and then discuss what they observed. An instructional coach can facilitate learning walks for teachers, other coaches, and administrators.

In formal rounds, descriptive language that is evidence-based from the observation, rather than judgment- or opinion-based, is used. Observers gather evidence on a specific problem of practice—a narrow focus the school has worked on—to share back with the staff. In one school where I worked, for instance, we had a clear focus on supporting English language learners to participate orally using academic language. When we did a version of instructional rounds at that school with a group of coaches, we created a note-taking guide that allowed us to track the language we heard students use as well as the strategies the teachers employed to support students in using academic language.

Learning walks and instructional rounds can be done with a group of site leaders, coaches, or teachers. When I worked in a district where each site had an instructional coach, I oversaw the professional learning and support of the coaches. I facilitated a version of learning walks to support their growth and development by forming groups of three to five coaches. I would pre-select the site where we would meet. Before the group meeting, I met with that school's coach and the principal to discuss the purpose and focus on the walk.

There were always a few purposes I wanted to achieve during these learning walks. First, I wanted our coaches to develop a common language in which to discuss teaching and learning practices. The only way to have a common language is to be together observing the same thing and then discussing what we observed. Second, I wanted to support those coaches who were lacking in instructional knowledge or coaching skills. The value of our group discussion was that each coach could hear others' perspectives on a common lesson observed. I strategically created the groups so that I had a range of coaches with different strengths and needs within each group. Finally, I wanted to make sure the school benefitted from the learning walk. Our focus when visiting classrooms was always determined by the site's focus and the needs of their students and staff. That way the data we gathered could serve as feedback for the site and fuel further discussions about next steps.

In my current role, I facilitate learning and equity walks for small groups of assistant principals as well as for all our principals. We also have sites within our district that are doing modified versions of these walks with teams of teachers from their own site. These walks have the same purpose and are driven by the needs of the site we are visiting.

On the day of a learning walk, all the participants arrive at the chosen school and meet for the opening discussion. The facilitator will welcome the group and explain the purpose. The site coach or instructional leader will then give a little background on the school and will describe the problem of practice or the focus for the day's walk. The facilitator will have determined ahead of time how participants will take notes, how many classrooms they'll visit, and how long they'll stay in each classroom.

If this is the first time a group has participated in something like this, it is important to explain that while the group will be visiting individual classrooms, the walk is not about any particular teacher; in fact, I will ask people to refer to the classrooms we visit as A, B, C, etc., instead of using the teachers' names. This helps alleviate stress on the part of the teachers, who are often nervous enough when a group of visitors enters their room. It is also important that the administrator informs the entire staff that a learning walk will be taking place on the campus before the day the walk happens.

Once the opening meeting has taken place, the group (or groups, if you have a large contingent broken up into manageable groups) visits classrooms according to a pre-arranged schedule. Participants take notes on the form provided. The facilitator may decide to hold a mini-debrief after exiting each class, ensuring the group is standing away from the classroom and any open doors, or the facilitator may decide to wait until all classrooms have been observed before starting to debrief.

When the group (or groups) return to the meeting room after the observation, the first step is for participants to review their notes and be prepared to make evidence-based statements about what they observed. One of the facilitator's jobs during the debrief is to ensure statements are not judgment- or opinion-based. The facilitator must listen closely, correcting language as necessary and helping the participants form evidence-based statements about the observations. I once heard an observer say, "I think the teacher was great. The kids were all engaged!" As the facilitator, I had to remind the group that "great" was a judgment word and that we wanted to avoid judgment language. I asked one of the participants to provide us evidence about what he thought "engaged" meant and what the students were actually saying or doing during our observation.

With clarification, he was able to say, "Twenty-four of twenty-four students had their iPads on and were viewing the teacher's slides." This is a very different statement than "all students were engaged." This can also lead to the group coming to a deeper understanding of their collective definition of key words such as *engaged*.

The debriefing concludes with the group leaving the school site with evidence-based statements of what was observed and questions to consider for possible next steps. But this is not the end of the learning walk. It is just as important to debrief the process. The final step is for the facilitator to ask the group to reflect on how they felt about the process and how they might apply this to their own context.

An instructional coach plays a vital role in facilitating learning walks; this is true whether the coach is a teacher leader or a site administrator. This process helps a group clarify common language and get clarity on instructional strategies. It also supports deeper discussions about how we are and are not yet meeting all students' needs. And once a learning walk is over, the next steps can be put into action by the instructional coach. This might lead to further professional development, a new book study, or individual coaching sessions with teachers.

WORKSHOPS

A third way in which an instructional coach can facilitate learning is through professional development workshops. When I served as a coach, my school had a minimum day every Wednesday, where students were dismissed two hours early, so teachers were given extra planning time. One Wednesday afternoon each month was dedicated to our staff professional learning. As the coach, I collaborated with the principal to support her vision for our staff learning. During these Wednesday workshops, we were able to share new instructional strategies, analyze our student data, read relevant research, and hold staff discussions about our site focus.

My goal when planning a workshop is always to consider the adults who will be in the room. Here are a few things I consider:
- Who is the audience?
- What is our purpose?

- What do the participants already know about the topic or focus?
- How long will we be together?
- Will we need to build in a break?
- How will I get the participants interacting?
- What kind of activity can we begin with to get people in the learning frame of mind? People often arrive at a meeting, and their minds are full of all the other things on their to-do lists. By beginning a meeting with a brief activity, you can help participants reframe their thinking to be intentionally focused for the learning. This can be a question such as "Share one item that is on your to-do list after this meeting and one item that was a success today."

Regardless of the format, facilitating professional development is an important aspect of the role of an instructional coach. In order to plan impactful PD, a coach must know his or her staff and have a clear goal in mind. Ideally, a coach can collaboratively plan these adult learning opportunities with a team of teacher leaders to ensure that the content will be meaningful for all participants.

CHOOSE THE COACH ADVENTURE

If you have just arrived from Chapter Twelve or from Chapter Nine and are curious about Mr. Fox's next PD plan, keep reading.

If you have just arrived from Chapter Eleven where Ms. Martinez and her team had created an elaborate plan to ensure they controlled their calendars (instead of being controlled by the calendar), or you've just arrived from Chapter Four where Ms. Martinez and her team are building teacher capacity, skip down to read below.

PRINCIPAL FOX

Principal Fox was finally feeling more confident in his instructional coaching abilities. He was visiting classrooms regularly and offering teachers with grade-level specific feedback. After providing similar feedback in many classrooms, Mr. Fox realized these topics could be addressed in his next professional development workshop.

Mr. Fox brought his instructional leadership team together for a planning session. Before sharing his ideas with the team, he asked the team for some feedback. He facilitated a discussion using the following questions as a guide:

- How has your team worked to address our school-wide initiatives since our last PD?
- What successes has your team had?
- What challenges have come up for your team lately?

By beginning with these questions, Mr. Fox was able to hear a lot about how the teachers were perceiving their growth and their areas of concerns. He was surprised that one team felt they were struggling with their English-learner supports, when their data was showing significant growth. He was also surprised that one team was proud of their parent engagement work because he hadn't been aware of anything they had done to engage parents. These leadership team meetings continued to open Mr. Fox's eyes to the importance of taking time to listen to his staff and hear how the work was progressing from their viewpoint.

After everyone had shared, Mr. Fox began to lead the group in a brainstorming activity for their upcoming professional development workshop. He reminded the group of the school-wide initiatives and clearly stated that their PD would have to align to those key areas. He also shared with the team some of his recent observations (in general, without naming specific teachers or classrooms). One teacher said, "Yes, our team has been comparing our feedback from you recently, and we realized that you were giving us all the same questions and ideas."

The teacher leaders and Mr. Fox went on to plan a workshop they felt would meet the teachers' current needs and help move the school closer towards supporting their English learners to develop and use academic language orally and in writing. One teacher stressed how important it would be to create a seating chart that split up grade-level teams, so teachers could interact in cross-grade-level conversations. The group agreed, which pleased Mr. Fox.

- To reflect on Mr. Fox's journey and your own coaching adventure, go to Chapter Thirteen: Where Did This Coaching Adventure Take You?
- If you haven't begun to follow Ms. Martinez's journey yet, go to Chapter Five: What Is a Coaching Theory of Action?

PRINCIPAL MARTINEZ

Ms. Martinez and her team have created a coaching system at their large high school. As they continue to work to develop teacher leaders, Ms. Martinez recognizes that she could help advance her work if she included more teachers in the learning process. Ms. Martinez meets with her site leadership team monthly. At their next meeting, she asks if anyone on the leadership team would be open to doing a learning walk with an assistant principal and her. She suggests that the purpose would be to build a common language around the site focus areas and to share the coaching dialogues they've begun. Ms. Martinez says a teacher can join her and the assistant principal during their prep period, where they would be paid for their time, or they could have class coverage during one of their classes. Five of the leadership team teachers agree to give this a try.

Ms. Martinez creates a schedule so that a different assistant principal is walking with her during each period of the day. She is using this as an opportunity to model for her assistant principals while also building teacher leadership capacity. After the small group visits a classroom for anywhere from fifteen to thirty minutes, they step outside and away from the room for a short discussion. During the discussion, Ms. Martinez asks her teacher leaders to describe evidence of their site focus in action in the classroom. She keeps the group focused on descriptive, evidence-based language to avoid judgment or opinions. She then asks if one of the teachers would be willing to do a role-play with her. She wants to model a coaching conversation for the group to hear, using the class they had just observed as an example.

For each period that day, Ms. Martinez is able to role-play a coaching conversation, so the teacher leaders are all able to better understand the entire process. By the end of the day, the teachers who had participated were sending her thank-you notes and asking when they and their peers could do another learning walk together. Ms. Martinez can feel the positive energy and wants to continue the momentum.

- To learn more about Ms. Martinez's next steps, go to Chapter Eight: How Can Lesson Study Support Coaching?

Chapter Eleven
WHAT DO COACHES NEED TO KNOW ABOUT TIME MANAGEMENT?

Time management is an oxymoron. Time is beyond our control, and the clock keeps ticking regardless of how we lead our lives. Priority management is the answer to maximizing the time we have.

−JOHN C MAXWELL

Time is something we never have enough of no matter our role. New coaches often struggle to maintain an effective and efficient calendar. The more organized your calendar, the more time you will have to do the important work you need to do as a coach. I truly believe that your calendar can save you time and keep you focused—*if it is organized for that purpose.* Three areas to consider regarding time management and instructional leadership coaching are your calendar, your email use, and your classroom visits.

CALENDAR
If your calendar needs some 911 support, look no further than these tips.
1. Use your calendar to tell the story of your coaching. Instead of large blank holes on your calendar, look ahead at the upcoming month and make a plan.

    »   Schedule classroom visits now, so they take priority.
    »   Write due dates for all important tasks on your calendar in the FYI section (explained below).

» Begin with the mandatory work (classroom visits, coaching sessions, coach and team meetings, supervision, etc.); schedule those before optional events.

» Make appointments with yourself to complete time-sensitive tasks. If I know I need to submit a coaching plan (or safety plan or fill-in-the-blank task) by Friday, I schedule time on Monday to work on the plan. I also schedule time on Tuesday or Wednesday to review my work or make revisions based on feedback, in preparation for the final deadline.

2. Work smarter, not harder! If you know your team needs and appreciates a reminder email before each team meeting, plan the time to write those emails. The emails can be pre-written and saved in your Drafts to be sent on the appropriate date. Be sure to add a reminder in your calendar on the appropriate date, so you send them (or use the delayed delivery option in Outlook or other email systems).

3. Don't be afraid of the recurring feature on your calendar. If you have a weekly, monthly, or annual meeting or task, schedule it to recur at the appropriate time. If you do this once for each recurring event, you will save time in the long run. If you keep missing the PLC meeting for the team(s) you support, schedule those as well.

» I also do this with staff birthdays and other culture and relationship-building events that are equally important for coaches.

4. Use the color-coding features to meet your needs. My calendar color code is as follows:

» Blue for mandatory meetings and events
» Green for informational events I will attend if I'm able or just need to be aware of
» Pink for private or personal events after work hours or on days off (This could be things like exercise, which, if not scheduled, often doesn't happen!)
» Yellow for staff schedules (My secretary enters the

vacation/leave days of my staff on my calendar as a yellow FYI.)

5. Use the "All day event" feature as an FYI. On most calendars, when an event is all day, it shows up at the very top of the day. I put FYI events and reminders in that section of my calendar, so they don't show up like appointments midday. These can include deadlines, birthdays, reminders, notifications of other things happening around the campus, department, or district, etc.

6. Give others access to view your calendar. My team and I share our calendars so that we can easily schedule team meetings without twelve unnecessary emails and to see where a team member is if he or she is out of the office when we are looking for him or her. As a coach, you can print your weekly or monthly calendar and hang it on your door so when teachers stop by to see you, they know where you are and when you are free. They can also use this as a sign-up for coaching sessions.

7. If you have support staff, give them access to view and edit your calendar. If you are out of the office, the staff who view your calendar can say to a visitor, "I'm sorry, she is in classrooms observing teaching and learning right now and is unable to meet with you. I'd be happy to schedule a meeting for you during _____ or _____ time."

   » Here's an important note for new leaders working with support staff for the first time: Take the time to sit down with your new support staff and go over how you want to use your calendar and what his or her role will be in its support. Be clear about how items are added to the calendar, what the color codes mean, and when and how changes can be made.

EMAIL

Email can be the bane of our existence. We need it, we love the speed and efficiency of it, but we also hate the volume and tediousness of it.

Most people in my life know that I hate to see that blue number above someone's email icon on their phone. When I see a number like 10,322 [unread messages], I start to sweat and have trouble breathing. I am proud to keep my Inbox under control (and under ten messages most of the time). While keeping your unread messages under ten might not be a priority to you, having an organized system can keep email from sucking up unnecessary energy. Here is how I manage my inbox:

1. Do not be a slave to that little "ding" on your computer or phone. To avoid reacting the minute you get a new message, turn off notifications from as many apps as possible—including email. Set aside specific times of day to read and respond to email. With an organized calendar (see above), you can schedule this time into your day as needed to get started. During your specific email-reading time, follow the tips below to achieve the smallest Inbox you've ever had.

2. When you read an email, make an immediate decision about it. If you need to respond . . .

   » Write the response and send it.
   » Write the response and save it in drafts to be sent later. (Be sure to make a note on your calendar about when to send it.)
   » Schedule time on your calendar to complete the response (and necessary research, collaboration, etc.).

   If you do not need to respond . . .

   » Delete the message. (If it is junk, unsubscribe or mark it as junk so it never reappears.)
   » Forward the message to the appropriate people.
   » File the message in the appropriate folder within your email system (see #3).

3. Create folders with your email based on the types of messages you need to save. Folders can be the names of people (your boss, your team, etc.), topics (schedules, Twitter, PLC, etc.), or events (Back to School, Open House, Coaching Cycles, etc.). They can also be task oriented (Do

This Week, Completed, Save for Reference, etc.). I know some people who use just one folder (Old Stuff), and when they need to find a saved message, they can search in that one folder. Folders are used to get messages you have dealt with—but need to save—out of your Inbox. Think carefully about what truly needs to be saved. Be aware that saving every message just creates cluttered electronic filing cabinets! See tip #4 for more about this.

4. Every six months, block out thirty minutes to go through your folders and archive or delete messages that you no longer need. In my school district, our email system has limited capacity, and our inboxes often get so full we can no longer receive messages. If I saved everything, I would never get another email again! While this may sound tempting, this can be quite damaging when you miss important tasks. Even if your system (like Google) has a much higher limit, I encourage you to do this. Email folders can be just like dusty file folders in filing cabinets: full of unwanted and unnecessary stuff.

5. Avoid the "reply all" nightmare email chain. When you are sending out a message to a large group (such as your entire staff or district), put your own name in the "To" line and then put everyone else in the "BCC" (Blind Carbon Copy) line. This way, even if someone hits "reply all" their message will only come back to you.

   » As a side note to this, if your colleagues are unfamiliar with email etiquette, as the leader, you are responsible for modeling this and supporting them in their learning. If your staff is known for inappropriate email banter, set the example with your emails and follow-up with individual face-to-face conversations.

6. Create rules for emails. In my office, we use Outlook, so it's easy to create rules to send certain emails directly into a folder. We get a daily message that says if our spam filter is holding any spam messages for us. Because I don't want these messages to clog up my Inbox first thing each

morning, I set up a rule, so they go directly to my Spam Filter folder. Later, when I have time and my important emails have been handled, I can check that folder to take action. I also set up rules for the ListServs I am on. I enjoy receiving and reading blogs and newsletters via email, but I like to read them on my own time. If they immediately go into a folder, my inbox is not overloaded, and I make time to read them at my leisure.

7. Be sure to delete your junk and deleted messages regularly. I also make a point to go through my Sent Mail regularly and delete many messages. I often save Sent Mail that is important (for documentation, reminders, support, etc.), but I get rid of all the minor messages exchanged throughout a week.

8. Do not ignore email. It will pile up and get unmanageable quickly without a system. If you are going on vacation (or will be out of the office for full-day workshops), schedule a response to be delivered to anyone who emails you, so they are aware of when you will return and respond. If you are overwhelmed, revisit your calendar and use that to schedule time to support your email responses.

MAKING TIME FOR CLASSROOM VISITS

As I work with new coaches and leaders, I often hear frustration and stress from them about their inability to get into classrooms as much as they would like. Coaches are often surprised at the amount of paperwork or non-coaching meetings they are required to attend. In addition to maintaining an organized and focused calendar and email system, there are some things you can do to make your time in classrooms efficient:

- Take your work out of the office and into classrooms. There are many leaders these days who have set up mobile desks in order to work anywhere on campus at any time.
  - » If you have a lot of low-thinking tasks to complete on your computer, consider if you can do them while sitting in the back of classrooms. Your presence will

be noticed, you will get work done, and you will see and hear learning in action.

» If you are an administrator with a pile of low-level discipline referrals on your desk that require you to speak to students, consider taking the referrals out to classrooms. Observe a classroom for a few minutes, then pull out the student with whom you need to speak. This gives you time to see the students in the class where they had an issue and then speak to them without them having to miss extra time out of class.

- Set a purpose for your classroom visits. New coaches will often find a free moment to leave their office, but when they get into classrooms, they aren't sure of what to do. When observing classrooms, a coach needs a purpose. Are you visiting in order to . . .

  » Look for evidence of a school-wide initiative or recent professional development (such as daily objectives or a student interaction strategy)?
  » Complete a formal or informal observation?
  » Provide the teacher with constructive feedback about teaching and learning?
  » Focus on English earners' participation?
  » Observe the students with the most behavior problems?
  » Observe for alignment to state standards and appropriate level of complexity?
  » Ensure teaching and learning are taking place?
  » Determine what percentage of class time students speak?
  » Prepare for a coaching cycle?
  » Follow up after a coaching cycle has been completed?
  » Observe a class in which a teacher is struggling and has asked for your support?

- Create a note-taking guide that aligns with your purpose. Based on all the different reasons listed above for which you might visit a classroom, what you write down to share with the teacher could be very different. It's important for a coach to be prepared to capture the appropriate data in order to provide evidence-based feedback. Here are some examples:

» When looking for school-wide implementation of a specific strategy, your goal may be to capture the total number of classrooms using the strategy and to what degree each room was implementing. You could then summarize this data for your staff without any teachers' names included. This could be captured on a table you create ahead of time or in a Google Form.

» When completing a formal observation, you typically need blank paper or a word processing document to write word for word (as much as possible) what the teacher and the students say.

» When visiting for general teaching and learning observations, it is best to select something specific to observe. In order to provide evidence-based feedback to teachers, having a narrow purpose and a clear note-taking guide helps. If you walk into a room without a purpose, your feedback may come across as disjointed.

Once you have a handle on your calendar, your email, and your purpose for being in classrooms, you need to create your coaching plans and schedule them. A coaching cycle, as discussed in a Chapter Six, is only successful if it is followed through from beginning to end and in a timely manner. If you, as a coach, begin a cycle and are unable to finish it, teachers will lose faith in your coaching abilities. They may be less willing to work with you in the future. And your impact on teaching and learning will diminish.

In any position, unexpected situations will arise. People will try to steal your time in a variety of ways. It is important for your coaching that you communicate clearly with those around you about the value you place on your instructional coaching time and the parameters under which it can be interrupted. Then you need to stand firm in following your calendar and not allowing other people's emergencies to distract from your focus.

As a coach (before the days of shared electronic calendars), I used to print my weekly and monthly schedule and hang it on my door so that if I was not in my office, people could see where I was. I also encouraged teachers to use this to sign up to meet with me or to schedule a coaching cycle for a later date. It was also a nice way to be able to justify my position to my principal whenever she had to ask our school site council to continue to fund the coaching position. My biggest priority as a coach was to interact in classrooms with teachers and students as much as possible. Coaches who never interact with students and teachers are ineffective. Be sure you are an effective coach by using your time wisely!

CHOOSE THE COACH ADVENTURE

If you have just arrived from Chapter Three and are curious about Mr. Fox's calendar issues, keep reading.

If you have just arrived from Chapter Five, where Ms. Martinez was trying to help her administrative team put their new coaching plan into action, skip down to continue her story.

PRINCIPAL FOX

Mr. Fox had just begun to visit classrooms, but he was quickly becoming overwhelmed by his calendar and to-do lists. Every time he left the office, his secretary would call him on the radio to ask a question or tell him someone was there to see him. When he returned to the office, there seemed to be a growing pile of things that needed his attention. He felt like he just couldn't keep up with the workload and his new visitations. He knew he didn't want to stop visiting classrooms, so he began to seek out professional advice, through books, blogs, and colleagues, about time management.

After reading as much as he could one weekend, he came into school the following Monday morning and pulled his two office secretaries in for a meeting. He explained to them that he was going to be visiting classrooms at least two mornings and one afternoon a week. He let them know what his purpose was and how important this was to his work as an instructional leader and the coach that the teachers deserved. The secretaries had questions about what their roles would be if students were sent to the office, if parents came in demanding to see him, or if an emergency occurred. As a team, they decided what would constitute an emergency and that they could radio or call his cell phone immediately in those cases. They created a plan for student discipline situations. Mr. Fox explained that he would be communicating his new schedule and priorities to the staff and to parents so that if someone dropped by to see him, the secretaries could refer to his message and schedule a meeting for another time.

Mr. Fox added the blocks of time for his three classroom visits to his calendar as a weekly recurring appointment. He gave both school secretaries access to view and add to his calendar, so they knew when to schedule appointments. He sent out a message to staff and parents to communicate his new schedule. There were some challenges at first as his secretaries learned how to communicate his expectations to people who confronted them and when other items came up that might cause him to skip one of his scheduled visits. But within a month, Mr. Fox felt like he was managing his time better than he ever had. He then began to really focus on what he was seeing in classrooms and what teachers were saying to him about his feedback.

- To learn more about Mr. Fox's challenges with giving feedback, go to Chapter Seven: Who Is Listening the Most?
- To learn more about Mr. Fox's initial steps into observing and coaching, go to Chapter Six: What Does Coaching Look Like?

PRINCIPAL MARTINEZ

Principal Martinez and her team had just established their coaching model and a plan to get into classrooms individually and together. They quickly realized, however, that it was hard to be in classrooms as much as they had planned. The assistant principals began to get bogged down with discipline issues in the office and walk-in parent meetings, and they were soon missing their individual classroom visitations.

While none of them missed the first-quarter learning walk the team had scheduled, there came a day when an assistant principal missed his scheduled visitation with Principal Martinez. At the next leadership team meeting, Principal Martinez brought up the issue of time management. After hearing the team's recent struggles, they worked together to brainstorm a few solutions.

- The weekly classroom visitation schedule would be shared publicly with the entire school staff through the principal's weekly bulletin. This would provide some added accountability for all involved. No one wanted to intentionally disappoint a teacher who was expecting a visit.

- In the next Coffee with the Principal and monthly newsletter to parents, Principal Martinez would communicate to parents about their new instructional coaching work. She would explain how important it was for all administrators to be in classrooms during learning time and how they would all be available to talk to and meet with parents during non-instructional times.

- The office staff, especially the secretary working with the assistant principals, would be coached on how to address walk-in parents, minor discipline issues, and other items sent to the office when the assistant principals were out visiting classrooms. They created a specific protocol with the secretary for when classroom observations should be interrupted (via the walkie talkie or a text message to the administrator) and when they should not be interrupted.

- The team also discussed their top ten frequent flyer students—the students most often sent to the office or involved in behavior issues. As a team, they reviewed those students' schedules and made sure that each day, at least one administrator would visit one of their classes and try to make a personal connection with each student (and see their behavior in class during informal observations). This was in addition to the work of the student study team (SST), where these students were being evaluated for additional supports and interventions.

As the team began to implement these new changes, they found success getting out of the office more than in the past. But one of their original issues came back up: Some teachers were still not engaging with them through the feedback process; in fact, some teachers were ignoring their feedback and avoiding meeting for face-to-face conversations. Principal Martinez's coach suggested the leadership team begin to discuss how they could build teacher leadership capacity within a core group of teachers.

- To learn about the team's next steps at Learning for All High School, go to Chapter Four: What Is the Role of a Teacher Leader as an Instructional Coach?
- To learn about Ms. Martinez's next idea for staff learning, go to Chapter Ten: How Do Coaches Facilitate Collaborative Professional Learning?

Chapter Twelve
HOW DO COACHES ADDRESS CHALLENGES AND ROADBLOCKS ALONG THE WAY?

Whether people perceive a change as positive or negative depends not only on the actual outcomes of the change, but also on the degree of influence they believe they exert in the situation.

–DARYL CONNER

No one wants to get mired in negativity. Coaching can be fun and exciting! As you embark on your journey to becoming a more effective instructional leadership coach, however, you need to be prepared for challenges. If unprepared, challenges can lead to permanent problems. But if you can anticipate the roadblocks, you will be better prepared to address issues that come up along the way.

The roadblocks you are likely to face will be determined by your position; for instance, if you are a teacher leader coaching other teachers, you might have to contend with peers who do not want to work with a coach or who are unwilling to try a new practice. Both teacher and administrative coaches might hear some version of "we've always done it this way" when trying to coach into a new, innovative idea that requires someone to step out of their comfort zone. You might work in a situation where you have limited support from your site or district leaders, making your coaching work an uphill battle. Or you could be in a system that believes that "fidelity to the textbook" is the expectation, which makes coaching conversations about pedagogy a challenge. One of the biggest frustrations you could face is seeing inequitable practices, live in action in your own school, that are not good for students.

While I can't prepare you for every obstacle that may appear before you, I can share with you some of the challenges I have faced and overcome as a coach in hopes that you can learn from my trials, tribulations, and successes. Jump into my coaching adventure for a few minutes and join me as I take you on a ride!

I DON'T WANT OR NEED COACHING

I once worked as a coach for the English department of a large high school. The department chair was a veteran staff member who made it clear to me that she did not need coaching, nor did she believe that I had anything to contribute to her department. She refused to include me on the department agendas, so as I got to know the team, I would attend those meetings as a silent observer.

At the same time, I began to build relationships with individual teachers. They invited me into their rooms to work with them, and we would have great discussions that led to coaching cycles based on their professional goals. Then I hit a department roadblock: the "Core Lit" list.

Many years prior to this, the department had come up with a list of core literature that they would teach, with certain novels or plays being assigned to each grade level, so students wouldn't read the same text in two different English classes. The list included *Romeo and Juliet* and *The Great Gatsby*, to name a few. The list did not include any text written within the last fifty years nor any text written by a person of color.

In one of my coaching cycles with a ninth-grade teacher, the teacher realized that the upcoming required "Core Lit" for his class was not a text with which his students would connect. He and I had worked through some behavior challenges with his students, and he was really focused on planning engaging lessons that met his students where they were as young teenagers, many of whom came from troubled backgrounds. I was proud of his realizations, but I knew that if he didn't teach the Core Lit, there could be backlash. As a coach, I did not tell him what to do. I asked him questions to help him make decisions. I asked him things like . . .

- Why do you think this text is on your grade level's Core Lit list?
- What other texts might meet the same expectations?
- What would happen if you used the Core Lit as expected?
- What would happen if you didn't use the Core Lit as expected?
- Is there anyone else in the department with whom you could talk about this?

After a number of conversations, this teacher felt comfortable bringing up his concerns with his ninth-grade PLC, with me present by his invitation. Two of his colleagues agreed with him, and we all had a lively discussion about possible next steps in their planning to meet their students' needs.

We later found out that another colleague, who had sat in that PLC meeting very quietly, did not agree with the discussion. She had gone to the department chair to explain what was going on in the ninth-grade PLC. The department chair came to me to demand an explanation as to why I was dismantling their "Core Lit" list. At first, I was flabbergasted, as this accusation came out of the blue to me. Then I realized how the story had gone from a PLC meeting to this, through the perspective of the one ninth-grade teacher with whom I hadn't yet developed a strong relationship. But at the time, I didn't know how to respond to this very angry department chair yelling at me about "Core Lit."

At that moment, I had a few choices. I could argue back with the department chair, defending myself and the actions of the ninth-grade team. I could share my personal opinion about the "Core Lit" list. I could apologize and back away from the issue entirely. But I chose none of those options; instead, I used the art of questioning to have a deeper conversation with this teacher.

"What concerns you?" I asked her.

"What do you mean?" she responded. She seemed taken aback by my calm question.

"I mean, what bothers you about the ninth-grade team's work or my role in the team planning?"

"Well, I believe that the district doesn't support our Core Lit list and that you were sent here to convince us to stop using it."

Wow. That honesty came out fast. If I hadn't taken the time to ask this teacher what her concerns were, I would have never truly understood the underlying fear. Once I heard it, I had a way to work with this teacher, explaining what my coaching role was and wasn't.

Not only do I constantly come back to asking open-ended questions when I face a coaching challenge, but I find that being fully honest and transparent about my work always helps alleviate concerns. Being able to explain what my coaching work is and is not has helped many people accept my role and even invite me in to collaborate with them over time.

This does not mean that we stopped talking about "Core Lit," but it does mean that the department chair invited me into meetings more willingly, asked for my opinion, and even volunteered her advanced class for a coaching cycle with me later in the year.

WE'VE ALWAYS DONE IT THIS WAY

Another challenge I have experienced as a coach is hearing some version of "We've always done it this way, and we don't need to change it now." As someone who loves trying new things, this attitude can instantly rub me the wrong way. But as a coach, I put aside my feelings and try to get to the root of what people are holding on to. Often I find people have a hard time articulating two thoughts:

- I don't know how to do what you are asking me to do, but if I admit that, I might feel stupid.
- I'm scared that I will fail, and I don't feel comfortable taking the risk.

If you can determine the root cause of people's fears and insecurities, you can help them overcome them and be willing to try something new. To do this, you must have trusting relationships with people; therefore, before I even think about offering my own suggestions or bringing up a big change idea, I work hard to get to know my teachers as individuals. I listen much more than I speak. I observe what they do, and I celebrate their strengths. If and when I do see them taking a risk, I honor and celebrate that too.

DEALING WITH INEQUITY

One of the biggest and most unexpected challenges I faced in my first coaching role was seeing practices—live and in action—that were not good for students in my school. Since my first coaching job was in the same school where I had been a teacher, I was working alongside people who had been on my team for years. We had planned together, sat in professional development together, and talked about our work together a lot. When I first went into some of their rooms, I was honestly shocked by what I saw. Some of the instruction was not only weak but actually ineffective and inequitable for students. But as a peer coach, it was not my job to judge or evaluate my peers. I was there to support our work and our literacy initiatives.

I struggled with recognizing my personal judgments and learning how to set them aside. I then had to learn to coach into conversations about equitable teaching practices in ways that invited my colleagues into the discussion without making them defensive. This is where I first realized how valuable an open-ended, reflective question could be. It was also how I learned the value of modeling.

As a new part-time coach, I knew I could use modeling as an effective coaching strategy in a couple different ways. One way was to invite teachers into my room during the times I was teaching my own students, so they could observe me. During my non-teaching periods, I was then able to model lessons or co-teach with other teachers in their classrooms. It's one thing to watch someone teach their own students well, but it's another to see a new strategy taught to your own students. My modeling in other teachers' classrooms allowed them to see that their students could learn new skills, could practice our initiatives, or could behave differently if the structure was provided. Modeling often led to the teacher and me co-planning and co-teaching follow-up lessons together as the teacher began to take on the new strategy in his or her own way.

So often I find that the best ways to address challenges are to be honest, to ask questions, and to be humble and vulnerable yourself. By putting myself out there as a teacher and a coach, I invited my peers to give me feedback about my teaching while we were exploring new strategies together. I have no problem admitting that I am not perfect, but to model a lesson that doesn't go well is a way to demonstrate that quickly! Not that I ever tried to bomb a lesson, but if it happened, I quickly called it a bomb, so the teacher and I could reflect and make a game plan for our next steps.

By now you may be sick of reading my reminders about taking time to build trusting relationships through listening, but there is a method to my repetitive madness. Without relationships, the challenges described above would have been even more difficult for me to get through as a coach. Even though I still met up with struggles throughout the process, my desire to presume positive intentions in others and to maintain positive professional relationships ensured that my coaching work was able to move forward. You may face similar challenges or problems that I have never heard of, but I promise you that if you start with building relationships, you will have a solid foundation for the more difficult work that follows.

CHOOSE THE COACH ADVENTURE

If you have just arrived from Chapter Five and are curious about Mr. Fox's staff meeting, or you've arrived from Chapter Two where Mr. Fox was struggling with how to give feedback to teachers, read on below.

If you have just arrived from Chapter Six where Ms. Martinez had just received a complaint about her assistant principal's work with a teacher during an attempted coaching cycle, skip down to continue her story journey.

PRINCIPAL FOX

We left Principal Fox struggling with his new attempts to be an instructional leader. He quickly realized that his teachers were unsure of his new role and that he needed to be more transparent about his own learning. At the next staff meeting, Mr. Fox shared his core values and his coaching beliefs. He asked the leadership team to come together to share their core values as well, which they were willing to do and to take back to their grade-level teams.

In his weekly update, he began to include a section about instructional leadership coaching. Each week, he would share a quote or an excerpt from his own professional reading on the subject, and then he would write his own reflection about the work.

He explained to his staff that as he was learning how to step into the instructional leadership coach role, he was still learning a lot, and he needed their help. He asked each grade level to come up with an instructional focus on which they were working, so it could help him narrow his feedback. When Mr. Fox began to give the teachers feedback on an area of their choosing, they were happy to see him enter their classroom whether it was once a week or once a day!

As Mr. Fox continued to align his feedback to the school focus and the grade level's chosen ideas, more teachers began to invite him into their rooms to see specific lessons; additionally, some teachers were feeling more comfortable approaching him after school to discuss the feedback he had provided. These brief conversations were leading to deeper levels of instructional coaching.

After a few weeks of this, Mr. Fox noticed that the feedback he was giving was very similar across all grade levels. He realized that it might be time to plan for the next PD opportunity and that his planning could be aligned to his observations.

- To learn about Mr. Fox's next steps in PD planning, go to Chapter Ten: How Do Coaches Facilitate Collaborative Professional Learning?
- To reflect on Mr. Fox's journey and your own coaching adventure, go to Chapter Thirteen: Where Did This Coaching Adventure Take You?

PRINCIPAL MARTINEZ

When we left Ms. Martinez, she had just heard a complaint from a teacher about one of the assistant principals. While Ms. Martinez's coaching cycle had gone well, the coaching cycles her assistant principals had tried were not as successful. Two of the assistant principals had moderate success, with the teacher tolerating the process for five days. In one case, the teacher tried on a new strategy with some success. In the case of the third AP, the AP stated that the learning cycle went "fine." The teacher, however, complained that it had not been very successful.

During a coaching cycle, the assistant principal had missed two of the scheduled planning sessions, had left the lesson early on two days, and at the end of the week, the teacher felt more frustrated and less clear about the instructional goal they had set together for the cycle. The teacher was not only annoyed with the assistant principal but was bad-mouthing the coaching cycle process to her peers, which was creating a challenge for Ms. Martinez, who was trying to develop support for a coaching culture on campus.

Ms. Martinez listened to the teacher, asked some follow-up questions, and spent time explaining the purpose of a coaching cycle.[1] After hearing the purpose and how it was supposed to work, the teacher realized that she wasn't annoyed with the process but with the delivery by one specific individual. Ms. Martinez asked the teacher to give her time to work with the assistant principal and encouraged the teacher not to share the negative experience with her peers.

Still unsure if the bad-mouthing would stop, Ms. Martinez next scheduled a meeting with the assistant principal. When she asked him how his first coaching cycle had gone, he said it was good. Ms. Martinez asked for more details, including what the focus was, and the assistant principal had a hard time responding. Ms. Martinez decided to be completely direct with him, explaining that the teacher had come to her to complain about the coaching cycle. She laid out the details of the complaint as well as her concerns about the impression he had left with the teacher about coaching cycles. At first, he argued with her, but finally admitted, "This is really hard." This statement created an opportunity for a dialogue about the challenges of being an assistant principal who is an instructional leadership coach. At the end of their meeting, Ms. Martinez was happy the assistant principal had felt comfortable enough to be honest with her, but she was still concerned about his lack of instructional abilities, and she was unsure what to do next to support him.

- To learn more about what Ms. Martinez does next with the assistant principal, go to Chapter Nine: Who Is in Your PLN?
- To learn more about Ms. Martinez and her teamwork to recover from the coaching cycle situation, go to Chapter Four: What Is the Role of a Teacher Leader as an Instructional Coach?

Part IV

Finding Your Coaching Adventure

Throughout this book we have followed the coaching adventures of the leaders from Smooth Sailing Elementary School and Learning for All High School. As we near the end of our coaching adventure together, I want to encourage you to take time to reflect on what you've learned and what you hope for in your own coaching journey.

CHOOSE THE COACH ADVENTURE

At this point in your reading adventure, whether you've been following Ms. Martinez or Mr. Fox, you are now here. I would like to encourage you to read these final chapters together. Imagine how Mr. Fox and Ms. Martinez would reflect on their journeys. Apply what you've learned from them to your own coaching journey. If you followed only one of the adventures, feel free to go back to the introduction and follow the second adventure for more learning.

Chapter Thirteen
WHAT IS YOUR COACHING ADVENTURE?

A coaching ADVenture begins with an *appreciation* of an individual's strengths. From there, a coach collaborates with his or her colleague to design a coaching plan that will help the educator transform his or her instructional practice on behalf of students. When completed, a coach has added value to a teacher's repertoire, and the duo can value and appreciate the work they did together. So the question for you now is, where do you want to add value? As a teacher leader, an assigned coach or mentor, or as a site or district leader, you have the potential to begin your own coaching adventure right now.

As I mentioned in the introduction, I see three paths on which you might be at this stage in your career. Each of these stages is ripe for a coaching adventure.

1. You are about to begin, or are in, a job that includes the role of instructional coaching.
2. You are a teacher leader who wants to improve your own practice and share your learning with others; you recognize that you and your colleagues aren't getting much coaching, and you want to do more.
3. You are a site or district leader who wants to take on more of an instructional coach role; you support instructional coaches within your system.

APPRECIATION

No matter your current stage, take a moment to appreciate your own strengths first. Consider what you are good at as a teacher, a coach, or a leader. What do you enjoy most about your work?

When you know your own strengths, you can start to coach and support others. Your first step might be to help others reflect on their own strengths. And you, as a coach, can point out the strengths you observe in your colleagues' work.

Our coaching adventure principals each had different strengths. Mr. Fox was a great listener and a kind soul who learned how to use that skill to bring teacher leaders into his professional development planning. Ms. Martinez was skilled at individual coaching, and she used that to build the coaching capacity of her assistant principals and to coach on a larger scale with PLC and lesson study work. Both instructional coaches learned to appreciate the good work of those around them. That appreciation built a foundation for their coaching relationships.

Challenge: Share a note of appreciation with someone else privately or with our community using #CoachADV.

DESIGN

As a coach, in any role, you want to design a plan. Your design begins with what your colleague is already doing well and on what he or she wants to work in order to have a greater impact on student learning. If you aren't in a formal role yet, consider designing a coaching plan for yourself.

- At what do you want to be more skilled in your current role?
- Are there professional resources you can read (such as this book) to learn more?
- Are there colleagues in other schools or districts doing the work you want to learn?
- Can you ask someone to observe you and offer feedback on a very specific area of your practice?
- Have you sought feedback on your work from others?

These are also the same questions you will consider when designing a coaching plan for someone else. The difference is that you won't be alone in the process! You want to design a plan in collaboration with the persons you are coaching, as they need to know and understand the process and the intended outcomes in their classroom.

Ms. Martinez worked with her own coach to design a coaching plan for her assistant principals. They each then worked with a teacher leader to coach up their own departments. The team also designed a coaching plan that would provide all teachers with regular feedback from the coaches. This design was a way to introduce a coherent structure for feedback to their high school. The walkthrough observation schedule design was shared with the entire staff through Ms. Martinez's weekly staff update.

Mr. Fox designed an individual coaching cycle with his upper-grade teacher. The design was based on the academic needs of the students and the professional needs of the teacher. The coaching cycle was designed to provide modeling and support to the teacher as he tried on a new skill. Mr. Fox also worked with his leadership team to design professional learning opportunities that would benefit his entire staff. This design was more complex and required even more of his listening skills to be successful.

Challenge: Share your coaching design with a colleague or our community using #CoachADV.

VALUE

Value comes from the inside and the outside. You want to add value to someone else's practice—or your own—through coaching. This is often an observable, external skill that is learned and applied with regularity in the classroom. After a coaching cycle, you also want to value what you did as a coach and reflect on your work to impact student learning through a coaching relationship with a colleague. This may be an entirely internal reflection process, but it is important because with each new coaching encounter, you can learn more about yourself as an educator, a coach, and an instructional leader.

Mr. Fox realized he had added value to his site's focus when he brought his leadership team together to reflect after their first professional development day. He also added value to his upper-grade teacher's practice through their coaching cycle. Mr. Fox is still reflecting on the ways he can add value to his primary-grade teachers through individual coaching, but he has learned a lot about himself as a teacher, a coach, and a leader throughout his coaching journey.

Ms. Martinez added value to her school through her individual coaching of teachers and her work with the administrative team, most of whom then went out and added value to the teachers they were coaching. Her school was adding value to their larger community through their #ObserveMe movement and their regular sharing of best practices on Twitter. Ms. Martinez has spent a lot of time reflecting on the power of their collective voices and is working with her team to enhance this work on behalf of their students.

Challenge: Share the value you've gotten from a coaching experience. Reflect on how you've grown as a teacher through coaching someone else. Tell us about it using #CoachADV!

If you've taken time to complete each of the mini-challenges listed above in your coaching ADVenture, you can begin to see the value you can add to our profession.

One of the best parts of being an instructional coach is the privilege of visiting the classrooms of many hardworking, dedicated educators. In the last school year alone, I visited more than four hundred classrooms. In my current work, it is an honor to be able to coach assistant principals on instructional coaching, as they have a direct impact on all those teachers I was able to visit last year. As you begin to plan out your coaching adventure, I encourage you to find a way to visit as many classrooms as possible. There are amazing things happening in classrooms all over the world. The more we can see and share these best practices, the more we can help our entire profession grow.

This is the time to consider your coaching legacy. What value do you want to add to student learning today? What about tomorrow? How can your coaching make an impact on future generations of students? A legacy stands tall long after we are gone. How will you begin to build a foundation for your own coaching legacy today?

As a learner, I have experienced coaching in a variety of ways throughout my life. As a child, my father took my brother and me skiing for the first time. He and my mom got my brother and me all the required warm clothing, and we rented the boots and skis for this first outing. My dad took us up the chairlift, and when we got off, he said it was time to ski down. I had not been given a single lesson and didn't have a clue what to do. He taught me the "snowplow," which was to make a pizza-slice shape of my skis so that I could semi-control my speed down the hill. My brother was a natural, sailing down the slopes without a care in the world. I was not a natural. When I fell, which happened pretty quickly, I was immediately hysterical; Dad calmly told me to get up. It was only when I was crying and unable to get myself up that he came over to try to explain to me what to do. My dad's version of coaching was experiential in nature: You learn by doing. This worked okay for the skiing part, but not for the getting up part. Without strong upper body strength, I couldn't figure out how to get myself up when I fell. So I began to ski as cautiously as possible to avoid falling, thereby avoiding the challenge of how to get up. If I did fall, I would have to pop off my skis, get re-situated, and get them back on, all while avoiding slipping further down the slope. As Brené Brown talks about in *Dare to Lead*, I needed to be taught how to get up when I fell so that I was willing to take risks. Without the skills to get up, I was so scared of falling that I was stuck in this cautious place where I refused to push myself, thereby not growing as a skier.

> "If we don't have the skills to get back up, we may never risk falling. If we are brave enough, often enough, we are definitely going to fall."
>
> –BRENÉ BROWN

After some frustration, my parents arranged for me to take a lesson on our next ski trip. The lesson was a completely different form of coaching from an expert in the field who knew how to break down the skill into smaller chunks for me to learn. When I learned how to get up, I was more willing to take risks that led to me falling. Falling while skiing was no longer the worst thing that could happen to me.

I learned from my dad and from my ski instructor during this time of life. As we continued to go on ski vacations as a family, I also learned through new experiences and by watching my daredevil brother carelessly throw himself down each hill with abandon. Many years later, when I learned that I could take skiing as a P.E. class in college, I jumped at the opportunity. I was placed in an advanced group, based on the skill set of others in the class. By then I had been skiing for at least ten years, so I was experienced, but I was definitely not an advanced skier. This class brought on a new coaching experience for me. Once again, I was taken to the top of a hill (this time much steeper and with moguls to survive) and was told to ski down. The instructor watched us during this first trip so that he knew how to coach us up from there. Being with other advanced students raised the expectations for my skiing and forced me to practice new strategies to improve.

The individual being coached plays a critical role in how the coaching will be received and if he or she will succeed.

Learning how to ski taught me many lessons, but I'm only now reflecting on the coaching that I experienced throughout my skiing life. I was coached by family members and virtual strangers, people with whom I had complete trust and people in whom I had to place trust quickly due to the nature of the work. I was provided modeling, hands-on experience, and small-group instruction. I was asked to challenge myself, and I was surrounded by people who could do the work better than I. Each of these experiences taught me something about myself and about skiing. I realize that there was no right or wrong way to coach someone to learn how to ski, but that the individual being coached plays a critical role in how the coaching will be received and if he or she will succeed.

Years later, I had a few really fun ski vacations with friends as an adult. I was so grateful to my father for taking me to that first mountain, to my mother for insisting I take a lesson, and to my family for all the skiing we did together. All the coaching I received gave me a skill I could transfer to any ski mountain in the world, surrounded by friends or family. What a gift!

Honestly, that is the gift I hope to give others when I am coaching them. I want educators to find the best version of themselves on behalf of the students we serve in schools every day. Becoming an instructional coach allows you to give this gift to others.

Chapter Fourteen
WHERE DID THIS COACHING ADVENTURE TAKE YOU?

Hopefully you have been following the coaching adventure of our two principals, Andrew Fox and Rachel Martinez, throughout this book. Mr. Fox had an incredible journey starting out as a leader who didn't see himself as an instructional coach at all to implementing individual feedback, coaching cycles, and purposeful professional development workshops in collaboration with his staff.

Ms. Martinez was an instructional leader without a coherent system when we met her. Her journey helped her create a coaching theory of action, a plan for her entire administrative team to be in classrooms regularly, opportunities to build teacher leadership capacity, and a lesson study experience that required the listening skills of a true instructional coach.

Whether you followed the book in order of their journey or in numerical order of the chapters, you have ended here. The final chapter. But where is here?

Here is the beginning of your instructional leadership coaching journey. Now is the time for you to take the tools provided throughout this adventure and apply them to your coaching context. Whether you are an administrator or a teacher, you are a leader, and you can be an instructional coach as well.

How you proceed into your own coaching ADVenture is up to you. Whatever that journey looks like, I encourage you to share what you try with our coaching community using the hashtag #CoachADV on Twitter.

If you haven't read through parts one and two of this book, I encourage you to hop back into the adventures of Principal Fox and Principal Martinez to learn along with them on their journeys. If you've already read the earlier parts, it's time to decide what is next for you. And if you think this is where I tell you what to do next, you haven't been paying attention. This is where I give you a lot of reflective questions to consider for your own growth. Only you can know and understand your current context and what your next steps can be.

- What is your current role?
- In which of the three stages listed in the previous chapter do you find yourself?
- What do you appreciate about your own skills as an educator, a coach, and an instructional leader?
- What design of coaching would you appreciate experiencing?
- Where do you want to add value?
- What will your coaching theory of their action be?
- Who is someone on your campus or in your district that you trust?
- How can you begin a conversation about coaching with a trusted colleague?
- If you've never been coached, how can you experience that before trying to coach others?
- How can you ask for feedback on your own goals?
- Who is in your coaching community?
- How can you participate in the #ObserveMe movement as a coach?
- How can you connect with other instructional coaches?

I hope that you have enjoyed your #CoachADV. The only way to coach like an instructional leader is to begin to do the work, so I encourage you to jump in wherever you are—right now!

Appendix A
NOTE-TAKING GUIDES

A1–SIMPLE NOTE-TAKING GUIDE FOR CLASSROOM OBSERVATIONS

Time	Teacher	Students

In this simple note-taking guide, the coach takes note of what the teacher says or does and what the students say or do. It is always helpful to note the time as well, as this can help you address pacing as well as the length of each talk opportunity or task.

A2–BEHAVIOR CONCERNS

Time	Student Disruption	Teacher Response

A coach could use this note-taking guide if a teacher was asking for support with some challenging student behavior. The coach would note which students called out, acted out, or disrupted the learning during the observation time as well as how the teacher responds to each disruption. The notes could then be used for a discussion with the teacher and to formulate a plan for next steps.

A3—TRACK THE TEACHER

This note-taking guide involves the coach coming into the observation with a diagram of the classroom already done on a paper (or a computer). During the observation, the coach can take note of where the teacher goes in the classroom; for instance, the coach can mark an X each time the teacher stops to talk and then draw a line from one X to another as the teacher moves around the room. This guide is valuable when a coach is working with a teacher on how the teacher is calling on students (and on whom), how the teacher is using the space in the room, or on behavior management techniques such as proximity.

References

Aguilar, Elena. *The Art of Coaching: Effective Strategies for School Transformation*. San Francisco: Jossey-Bass, 2013.

Buckingham, Marcus and Donald O. Clifton. *Now, Discover Your Strengths*. New York, NY: The Free Press, 2001.

Burgess, Shelley and Beth Houf. *Lead Like a Pirate: Make School Amazing for Your Students and Staff*. San Diego, CA: Dave Burgess Consulting, Inc., 2017.

Couros, George. *The Innovator's Mindset*. San Diego, CA: Dave Burgess Consulting, Inc., 2015.

DuFour, Richard and Robert J. Marzano. *Leaders of Learning: How District, School, and Classroom Leaders Improve Student Achievement*. Bloomington, IN: Solution Tree Press, 2011.

Fullan, Michael. *The Principal: Three Keys to Maximizing Impact*. San Francisco, CA: Jossey-Bass, 2014.

Hirsh, Stephanie and Tracy Crow. *Becoming a Learning Team: A Guide to a Teacher-Led Cycle of Continuous Improvement*. Oxford: Learning Forward, 2018.

Knight, Jim. *Better Conversations: Coaching Ourselves and Each Other to Be More Credible, Caring, and Connected*. Thousand Oaks, CA: Corwin Press, 2016.

McGrath, Valerie. "Reviewing the Evidence on How Adult Students Learn: An Examination of Knowles' Model of Andragogy." *Adult Learner: The Irish Journal of Adult and Community Education*, 99–110. 2009. https://eric.ed.gov/?id=EJ860562.

Osterman, Karen F. and Robert B. Kottkamp. *Reflective Practice for Educators: Professional Development to Improve Student Learning*. Thousand Oaks, CA: Corwin Press, 2004.

Robinson, Viviane. *Student-Centered Leadership*. San Francisco, CA: Jossey-Bass, 2011.

Tschannen-Moran, Megan. *Trust Matters: Leadership for Successful Schools*. San Francisco, CA: Jossey-Bass, 2004.

Wenger, Etienne. *Communities of Practice: Learning, Meaning, and Identity*. New York, NY: Cambridge University Press, 1998.

Zander, Rosamund Stone and Benjamin Zander. *The Art of Possibility: Transforming Professional and Personal Life*. New York, NY: Penguin Books, 2002.

Interested in
Working with Amy?

Amy is a skilled facilitator, leading teams through mission and vision development as well as engaging professional development. Amy loves to collaborate with site and district leaders to design professional learning experiences that are meaningful and relevant for participants situated in their own unique contexts. Below are a few topics on which Amy is available to present or consult:

- Instructional Coaching
- Lesson Study
- Instructional Rounds/ Learning Walks
- Aspiring Leader Pipelines
- Curriculum Design
- Balanced Literacy
- Professional Development for Teachers, Aspiring Leaders, Site and District Leaders

About the Author

Amy Illingworth, EdD, is a lifelong educator, a learner, a coach, and a leader. Her leadership vision is to create equitable learning opportunities where student and adult learners thrive.

She has served as a teacher, literacy coach, and an administrator at the elementary, middle, and high school levels and has taught at the graduate school level. She currently serves as the assistant superintendent of educational services in the Encinitas Union School District in California.

You can connect with Amy on Twitter (@AmyLIllingworth) or on her blog reflectionsonleadershipandlearning.wordpress.com. She looks forward to interacting with you through the #CoachADV hashtag.

More from

DAVE BURGESS
Consulting, Inc.

Since 2012, DBCI has been publishing books that inspire and equip educators to be their best. For more information on our DBCI titles or to purchase bulk orders for your school, district, or book study, visit **DaveBurgessConsulting.com/DBCIbooks.**

MORE FROM THE *LIKE A PIRATE*™ SERIES
- *Teach Like a PIRATE* by Dave Burgess
- *eXPlore Like a Pirate* by Michael Matera
- *Learn Like a Pirate* by Paul Solarz
- *Play Like a Pirate* by Quinn Rollins
- *Run Like a Pirate* by Adam Welcome

LEAD *LIKE A PIRATE*™ SERIES
- *Lead Like a PIRATE* by Shelley Burgess and Beth Houf
- *Balance Like a Pirate* by Jessica Cabeen, Jessica Johnson, and Sarah Johnson
- *Lead beyond Your Title* by Nili Bartley
- *Lead with Culture* by Jay Billy
- *Lead with Literacy* by Mandy Ellis

LEADERSHIP & SCHOOL CULTURE
- *Culturize* by Jimmy Casas
- *Escaping the School Leader's Dunk Tank* by Rebecca Coda and Rick Jetter
- *From Teacher to Leader* by Starr Sackstein
- *The Innovator's Mindset* by George Couros
- *Kids Deserve It!* by Todd Nesloney and Adam Welcome

- *Let Them Speak* by Rebecca Coda and Rick Jetter
- *The Limitless School* by Abe Hege and Adam Dovico
- *The Pepper Effect* by Sean Gaillard
- *The Principled Principal* by Jeffrey Zoul and Anthony McConnell
- *Relentless* by Hamish Brewer
- *The Secret Solution* by Todd Whitaker, Sam Miller, and Ryan Donlan
- *Start. Right. Now.* by Todd Whitaker, Jeffrey Zoul, and Jimmy Casas
- *Stop. Right. Now.* by Jimmy Casas and Jeffrey Zoul
- *They Call Me "Mr. De"* by Frank DeAngelis
- *Unmapped Potential* by Julie Hasson and Missy Lennard
- *Word Shift* by Joy Kirr
- *Your School Rocks* by Ryan McLane and Eric Lowe

TECHNOLOGY & TOOLS
- *50 Things You Can Do with Google Classroom* by Alice Keeler and Libbi Miller
- *50 Things to Go Further with Google Classroom* by Alice Keeler and Libbi Miller
- *140 Twitter Tips for Educators* by Brad Currie, Billy Krakower, and Scott Rocco
- *Block Breaker* by Brian Aspinall
- *Code Breaker* by Brian Aspinall
- *Google Apps for Littles* by Christine Pinto and Alice Keeler
- *Master the Media* by Julie Smith
- *Shake Up Learning* by Kasey Bell
- *Social LEADia* by Jennifer Casa-Todd
- *Teaching Math with Google Apps* by Alice Keeler and Diana Herrington
- *Teachingland* by Amanda Fox and Mary Ellen Weeks

TEACHING METHODS & MATERIALS
- *All 4s and 5s* by Andrew Sharos
- *Boredom Busters* by Katie Powell
- *The Classroom Chef* by John Stevens and Matt Vaudrey

- *Ditch That Homework* by Matt Miller and Alice Keeler
- *Ditch That Textbook* by Matt Miller
- *Don't Ditch That Tech* by Matt Miller, Nate Ridgway, and Angelia Ridgway
- *EDrenaline Rush* by John Meehan
- *Educated by Design* by Michael Cohen, The Tech Rabbi
- *The EduProtocol Field Guide* by Marlena Hebern and Jon Corippo
- *The EduProtocol Field Guide: Book 2* by Marlena Hebern and Jon Corippo
- *Instant Relevance* by Denis Sheeran
- *LAUNCH* by John Spencer and A.J. Juliani
- *Make Learning MAGICAL* by Tisha Richmond
- *Pure Genius* by Don Wettrick
- *The Revolution* by Darren Ellwein and Derek McCoy
- *Shift This!* by Joy Kirr
- *Spark Learning* by Ramsey Musallam
- *Sparks in the Dark* by Travis Crowder and Todd Nesloney
- *Table Talk Math* by John Stevens
- *The Wild Card* by Hope and Wade King
- *The Writing on the Classroom Wall* by Steve Wyborney

INSPIRATION, PROFESSIONAL GROWTH & PERSONAL DEVELOPMENT

- *Be REAL* by Tara Martin
- *Be the One for Kids* by Ryan Sheehy
- *The Coach ADVenture* by Amy Illingworth
- *Creatively Productive* by Lisa Johnson
- *Educational Eye Exam* by Alicia Ray
- *The EduNinja Mindset* by Jennifer Burdis
- *Empower Our Girls* by Lynmara Colón and Adam Welcome
- *The Four O'Clock Faculty* by Rich Czyz
- *How Much Water Do We Have?* by Pete and Kris Nunweiler
- *P Is for Pirate* by Dave and Shelley Burgess
- *A Passion for Kindness* by Tamara Letter
- *The Path to Serendipity* by Allyson Apsey
- *Sanctuaries* by Dan Tricarico

- *Shattering the Perfect Teacher Myth* by Aaron Hogan
- *Stories from Webb* by Todd Nesloney
- *Talk to Me* by Kim Bearden
- *Teach Better* by Chad Ostrowski, Tiffany Ott, Rae Hughart, and Jeff Gargas
- *Teach Me*, Teacher by Jacob Chastain
- *TeamMakers* by Laura Robb and Evan Robb
- *Through the Lens of Serendipity* by Allyson Apsey
- *The Zen Teacher* by Dan Tricarico

CHILDREN'S BOOKS
- *Beyond Us* by Aaron Polansky
- *Cannonball In* by Tara Martin
- *Dolphins in Trees* by Aaron Polansky
- *I Want to Be a Lot* by Ashley Savage
- *The Princes of Serendip* by Allyson Apsey
- *Zom-Be a Design Thinker* by Amanda Fox

CPSIA information can be obtained
at www.ICGtesting.com
Printed in the USA
FSHW011906111019

9 781949 595871